# MERLIN ON MANSTONE MILL

Priest-Monk Silouan

*Father Silouan*

Stiperstones Press

2015

First published by the Stiperstones Press in 2015.
It is available from the printer, Lulu.com.
www.lulu.com

And from the Stiperstones Press,
Monastery of Saint Antony and Saint Cuthbert, Gatten, Pontesbury, Shropshire,
SY5 0SJ United Kingdom.

Monastery website: www.orthodoxmonastery.co.uk

Email: Silouan@orthodoxmonastery.co.uk

Telephone: 44 (0) 1588 650571.

# CONTENTS

# 1

# TALIESIN'S RETURN

Once upon a time, Taliesin the Bard returned from Byzantium, to abide with Merlin the Wise in a forest clearing known as Goatshaw Ring, under Wolfstone Tor, on the eastern face of the hill of Manstone Mynd.

Merlin had fled here from the forests of Caledonia in the north, to escape the ravages of war between Picts and Britons and the invasions of Angles from the east. Merlin's sister, Ganieda, was Cumbria's widowed queen. On the death of Rhydderch, her king, she had joined Merlin in the north and withdrew with him into the Caledonian wilderness. She came south with the Sage to Manstone Mynd, a quartzite hill of jagged tors, in the district of Pengwern.

Here, Brochwel reigned from Caer Guricon, white city of the woods, which Roman Cornovians called Viroconium, and Saxons, Wroxeter. Here, they had been joined by Maeldin, recently cured of a deranged mind, and Nimue of the Lake, exiled from Sarras, City of the Grail. Here, too, lived Dindrane of the Grail, sister of Percival, Knight of the Round Table.

Taliesin had been deeply inspired by Byzantium, founded by Constantine, Roman Emperor from Britain. Northerners called the city Micklegarth and the Byzantines Constantinople. Constantine's mother, Helen, came from Camelodunum, the City of Colchester, Roman Chester on the Cole, which guarded coastal access to the east. Some Cornovian Britons saw Byzantium, Constantine's City of Sophia, as their own beloved city in the east, retaining many ancient links that bound Britain to Byzantium. Taliesin was eager to share with Merlin the wisdom song that had been transmitted to him in the Great City, not to mention the news of a rich kingdom further east, and its Priest King, Prester John, who ruled in India.

Goatshaw Ring was an earth bank palisade enclosing wattle round cells, huddled beneath Wolfstone Tor. Seven turfed cells opened to clear views over the forest wilderness of Pengwern. Oak and ash, hazel and alder filled the valleys between the hills, where once the ice had lain. Merlin had chosen this place because it lay above fissures in the shales where great waters flowed, and healing came from hidden springs, on the dragon-spine ridge of Manstone Mynd.

The Manstone rocks ran like a serrated dragon's back extending from the northeast to southwest, at the heart of the Pengwern hills. Here forests thinned to craggy heath, littered with tors of broken quartz and rugged screes, shattered relics of the Age of Ice. Stone stripes, like dragon scales, scarred upper slopes beneath the steeple stones, and paired screes in elemental lines resolved into polygonal shapes and level plates lower down.

These screes drew down dragon's breath of creeping mist, retracing the shores of long-forgotten seas.

Manstone Tor was named after a stone to its north that looked like a Man, the Man Stone King. It was said he was a Lord of Wisdom, about whom Merlin knew, turned long ago to stone. Another was Wolfstone Tor, which some called Shepherd's Rock, for shepherds of wisdom used to gather there. It was said that councils of elders and sometimes seers would meet there, and listen to prophecies of kings, whose glory was long gone, or whose glory was still to come.

Nestling beneath Wolfstone Tor, Goatshaw Ring lay not far distant from the Throne, greatest of the tors, and axis of many intersecting worlds. Merlin knew this tor as the Throne, but Mordred called it the Devil's Chair. Morgana used to say that a Dark Lord was in residence there when mists descended and cloud shrouded the Throne.

Mordred's forces had broken the Sacred Circle of the Round Table, tearing land and people apart. He had felled King Arthur at the Battle of Camlann to the south, and left him bleeding with a terrible wound. Pierced by Arthur's Excalibur, sword of glory, Mordred himself passed into the shadows that only Merlin knew. Arthur, tended lovingly by three Ladies of the Lake, was in Avalon, a timeless sanctuary, hidden beyond vast waters and encircling mists, enshrouding untold worlds.

The powers that, through Mordred, had wrought ruinous confusion and cruel division had not died with him. The insinuations that seduced Morgana still lurked beneath the hills, working dark enchantment, consumed by envy of Merlin's wisdom and jealousy of Taliesin's chant. Despising Nimue's serenity and Dindrane's burning love, they schemed and plotted to hinder Taliesin's return. To them, Byzantium was a flame that burned, a light that pained their sight, hated because too bright. Subtle powers waited in hiding, unable for a time to challenge the wisdom of bard and mage. The Ring of the wisdom shepherds held firm.

Taliesin was strong in wisdom song, which was why he was remembered as the bard of the radiant eye. He was master of inkling vision, the half-guessed hint and dazzling metaphor. For him, poetic symbols leaped over faults and fissures that otherwise would tear apart the whole. They connected the world of sense with the netherworld of spirit. His wisdom songs were able to create what he saw, like crystallized sound, resonant and resplendent.

He had gone to Byzantium at the insistence of Merlin, who had heard that there was great wisdom in the City of Sophia, where the Emperor Constantine had adopted a Solar Cross for the banners of Rome's legions. The Emperor from Britain chose the Rood for his standard, and fought in the Name of anointed wisdom that some thought new, but others knew was older than the hills.

4

Taliesin knew the ancient wisdom of the Druids and the Groves of Oak. He was familiar with the hallowed wisdom of the Healing Henge, and the older wisdom of the Barrows and ever-present watchers, elders of the land. Merlin chose him because Taliesin could discern wisdom when he found it. It was Merlin's hope that Taliesin would be able to discern the wisdom of Byzantium and recognize how it wove with all that went before.

Mother Ganieda welcomed Taliesin's return most warmly. Her sorrowful mourning for the loss of all she loved, was easing now, here among the aching oaks. When Merlin came south to Goatshaw Ring, she came too, gently mothering everything. For Ganieda, Manstone Mynd was a haven of light, even though she was aware of shadows in the forest, lurking powers, shunning light.

Thunderstorms would encircle the tors, drawing lightning to the quartz. Mists would brood here, but sometimes the Man Stone would stand above it all, like an island king, surrounded by seas of cloud. Then hills were sunlit islands amidst ancient seas, waters of a forgotten past made visible again to seers who see.

As for Nimue, Lady of the Lake, she hoped that in Byzantium Taliesin would hear news of Sarras, City of the Grail. Perhaps elders dwelt there with wisdom from the east which, taken to heart, and practised, would unveil the Grail again. Dindrane had given her life's blood to see the Grail, and help her beloved brother, Percival, in his great quest.

Contrary to rumour and romance, Dindrane had not died, but was dead to the world here, before she died. Her reputed death was this desert wilderness on Manstone Mynd, where her heart of love found love for wisdom. Merlin's wisdom sustained her vision, and mirrored the Grail that seeing sees.

Nimue and Dindrane had been remembering Taliesin every day, one spirit with his spirit, as he journeyed east and back again. Both knew the Grail was like an empty chalice, empty as Ceridwen's fay cauldron of old, so they emptied themselves of themselves every day, like rings and crowns, torques and bands that trace the void which they surround.

For Maeldin, Byzantium might be a city of wisdom, but it was far away. It was the wise waters of the Manstone Spring that were healing his troubled mind. He took empty pitchers to its healing source every day, drinking from its bubbling purity to ease his soul. Somehow, he knew in his heart that whatever it might be that Taliesin found in Byzantium, it would be for him the bluestone waters that were healing him.

So Maeldin was content to prepare the meal whilst the others greeted and embraced. He was happy to remain silent as the others laughed and talked. He was glad to see their joy, for he had not forgotten Morgause's poisons that had driven him out of his mind. Maeldin had eaten poisoned apples, apples that had been meant for Merlin, and the deadly venom, for a while, had deranged him. He had fled to Merlin, who had brought him to the Manstone Spring, and with Ganieda's help he drank long and deep. His cure had been gradual, but to his joy they offered him a round cell in Goatshaw Ring, so he stayed.

Maeldin had been named after Mael Duin, the Irish voyager, but nobody had ever told him why. Voyages were not for him, so he was relieved that Merlin's choice for the journey had been Taliesin. Maeldin's place was here with Merlin, and Ganieda was like a mother to him. He was fond of old tales of questing, and loved the tattered book that Blaise had given to Merlin before he died.

Blaise had been Merlin's elder, so it was through him that Merlin had imbibed old wisdom. It was through him that its unfathomable mysteries had been transmitted. Handed on from heart to heart, by word of mouth, Blaise knew that wisdom was not bookish, but he hoped his book might remind those who were in danger of forgetting.

Wisdom shepherds, like Merlin, were not bookish, but Maeldin loved the book that spoke with love of the wisdom they both loved. Nobody knew what happened to Blaise's book, but Geoffrey of Monmouth once described an old book he saw. In his Life of Merlin, he tells of Taliesin and Merlin, Ganieda and Maeldin, but does not mention Dindrane, Nimue, or Byzantium.

Some say Merlin dictated Blaise's book, and that the seer was persuaded to recall his memories of Arthur's Commonwealth, his mysterious birth, the sword in the stone, the round table and its knights, and the tales they told. Perhaps Maeldin did not want the Book of Blaise to end with Arthur's wound. It could have been Maeldin who first told the story of Merlin on Manstone Mynd, and wrote about it later in that same book. Maybe that is how we come to hear of Taliesin's return from Byzantium and can listen to his wisdom song, which is a song of the Holy Name. Wisdom opened the eyes of the blind in Pengwern, transmitting the light of the quartz from the heights of Manstone Mynd.

# 2

# WISDOM SONG OF TALIESIN

The wisdom cell was a steep-roofed round house at the heart of Goatshaw Ring. Its wattle walls were intertwined with ivy and its turf roof swathed in wild woodbine. Its little windows peeped out over the forest from a soaring interior space, at the heart of which there was a raised hearth and central fire. The door was carved with the tree of life, as above, so below. Its seven bands were symbols of wisdom's seven heavens, as were wisdom's seven pillars, rough hewn from pine, cut from the surrounding woods, to support the dome. Between the pillars, seven arches enshrined one of wisdom's seven lamps, and it was here that Merlin lit the fire to welcome Taliesin from Byzantium.

A belfry to the south of the wisdom cell housed an old bell, salvaged by Bedivere from Camelot, and given by him to Merlin when Mordred's insurrection had torn the sacred land apart. Merlin tolled the bell, which reminded him of golden times now gone. Taliesin came with Ganieda, revered Mother in the Black Cloak, and Nimue in a flowing shawl of blue linen, and Dindrane in warm Hebridean weave. Maeldin wore his worn brown habit of rough wool, and Merlin the pure white garment of elders of old. Taliesin was wearing the Bard's Cloak of fine feathers, like eagle's wings, its many hues glistening and shimmering in the light of the fire. He had changed his mudded travelling clothes for the sacred garment of the bard, as was fitting, for his ancient office was revered here, as was the wisdom of the Barrows and the Healing Henge.

Merlin was seated to the right of the door, facing the ark and the altar behind. He waved to Taliesin to be seated to his right, Mother Ganieda and the sisters to the left, and Maeldin next to the carved cask of dry logs. Merlin sat poised and silent, turned within, seeing far into the dancing shadows. The glow of the flames rose like incense into the raftered dome above.

Suddenly, when the moment was right, Taliesin began to chant to a strange uneven rhythm and in unfamiliar mode. Alight with wisdom song, he was always bard to the core, allergic to traveller's chatter. He began to chant the Song of the Name, strange but familiar, known but new, freshly re-wrought in the furnaces of Old Byzantium.

So with lyre in hand he sang.

I came to tell thee my Name:

I am 'I AM' in thy midst.

Turn, turn, and thou shalt be turned;

turn and see who sees.

I am 'I AM,' that is my Name,

the glory belongs to God alone.

Vain, vain the glory when confusion reigns

and glory darkly falls.

Glory belongs to thy King.


I am 'I AM,' thy God.

'I AM WHO I AM,'

whispering in every heart,

stillness singing, burning, boundless love.

I am 'I AM,' calling thee by Name.

I am 'I AM,' thy heart my throne,

light sanctuary within, angels' chant.

Why, O why dost thou turn away?

Who will hear my song?


Calling, calling, without end,

prayer, without ceasing, in every heart,

yearning to be known, loved home.

God calls, gently seeking thee:

Give me back the Name 'I AM,'

and glory will to glory raise thee.

I am 'I AM,' light gives thee light.

Hallow my Name aright, O earth,

and heaven receives thee everywhere.


God's Kingdom comes when 'I AM' reigns,

not thee, usurping me,

confusing thyself with thy King.

Turn, turn, turn and see!

Nothing created here,

nearer than near:

'I AM' in the midst of thee.

Glory falls short when 'I AM' is confused,

division rules when confusion reigns,

'I AM' is 'I AM,' not thee.


Taliesin fell silent and laid his lyre aside.  He waited as the opening Word in the words sank in.

Nimue was the first to speak, she whose exile from Sarras, City of the Grail, had become a finely tuned alignment, awake to whispers beyond words.

'So, does this transmission of the Name 'I AM' convey the wisdom of the summer stars?' asked Nimue.

'Is this the 'I AM' of Bardic Lore? Is it the 'I AM' that shifts from shape to shape as does Ceridwen's fay cauldron of regeneration and inspiration?'

Taliesin, silent, nodded with a smile, carefully observing the light in her eyes, the delight that shone in her eager face.

'The wisdom, then,' she said, 'begins with "turn and see!" You have brought us the healing wisdom of Byzantium.'

Nimue, quick as lightning, saw straight through to the heart of the matter, the Matter of Byzantium.

'What of the Holy Grail?' she asked. 'Did they know of the Grail in Byzantium? What of the Matter of Britain?'

Taliesin answered slowly, aware that Dindrane was tense, all heart, on fire with love for the wisdom in the words. Addressing Nimue, in a low voice, he began to speak.

'I spoke with many in Byzantium, and there was one there who came from Jerusalem, who was from the family of the Arimatheans. They were heirs to Joseph, who was given the Grail by Pilate on Rood Friday. The Arimathean said there were members of his family dwelling even now in the British Isles, living in Carbonek, the Castle of the Fisher King. Some say the Grail is no longer there, but has been withdrawn to Sarras. Others say that Merlin hid it far away, with other treasures, concealed in the depths of a cave on Ynys Enlli, Bardsey Isle.'

Taliesin paused, as all eyes present turned their gaze on Merlin, who was staring into the embers, as if he was trying to remember something, or to forget something he no longer wanted to remember.

Slowly, with a shake of the head, barely discernible, Merlin spoke.

'Too often knights would seek the Grail as if it were somewhere, or despair of it, as if it were nowhere. They would go in search of it, like Percival, your brother, Dindrane, and think it was their own purity that mattered, forgetting the light that is never defiled, and the glory the light reveals. When they were disappointed, they despaired of their quest, or of themselves, apparently unaware that what they sought was always already present in their midst. Percival failed to ask both questions, "Who serves the Grail?" and "Whom does the Grail serve?" In any case, they failed to notice that the Secret of the Grail lies hidden in the loving heart of its first keeper, Joseph of Arimathea. Nicodemus had known this, for it had inspired his Gospel. But in the frenzy of quests, the love in Joseph's heart had been forgotten.'

Merlin turned to Dindrane, whose eyes were filled with tears.

'I have spoken to you of this many times, Dindrane, and you took this word to heart, as we all know.'

Dindrane looked uneasy, as if she was reluctant that they should think too well of her, instead of recognizing that the love she carried in her heart was inspired from beyond herself and was not hers, though hers by grace.

'The love in Joseph's heart was not his,' she said, 'and yet was his because he was not, like Enoch of old.'

Dindrane spoke in a strong clear voice, which communicated directly to the hearts of her companions:

'Do not think there is anything special about me. The 'I AM' is God's 'I AM,' not me. This love is proclaiming what Taliesin's Song just sang. My brother, Percival, thought I died when I gave my life's blood for him and his quest for the Grail. I am alive as you see, but he was not wrong. Something of me died then, and it was this that led me here. It was this that brought me to you, Merlin, or was it the wisdom that I see in you, awakening the seer in me?'

Nodding, Merlin turned to Taliesin, and gazing, said to him:

'The Song of the Name that you sang just now is, as I thought, a wisdom complete and well rounded. I am assured that we can embrace this wisdom of Byzantium with a whole heart, and through it include all that we have received from our elders, the wisdom of the Oaks and of the Healing Henge, and so fulfil the wisdom of the Barrows and the elder days, and the older wisdom of the Hunt. We may embrace the wisdom of the City of Sophia, and receive its ancient mysteries. As Nimue reminds us, it is a turning and a seeing, a doing and a knowing, which together give access to the hallows and their hallowing.'

'But what of the powers?' said Maeldin.

He had been silent until now, but intently listening. Now, he spoke.

'The powers confuse. The powers divide. I have known this terrible ambivalence, and it drove me out of my mind. It was the powers, Merlin, that were at work in the wars that drove you mad, and to escape their clutches, you fled to the forests in the north, after the battle of Arthuret Field. You fled again from Caledonia, came here to Goatshaw Ring, and with Ganieda's help, brought me to find healing in the Manstone Spring.'

'The wisdom of Byzantium speaks much and often of the powers,' said Taliesin. 'I spoke to many elders there, who called this the wisdom of Chalcedon, after a General Council held some years before, which spoke of the mysteries of God made man, without confusion or division, unveiling a wisdom of co-inherence that undoes confusion and heals division. They said they had devoted many long years to the Matter of Co-inherence, and assured me that we may put this wisdom to the test in countless ways and that it holds true.'

'But does this wisdom really heal?' asked Maeldin. 'If it does, how does it fit with healing wisdom springs that we know can heal?'

Maeldin's question was searing for him, and very close to the bone, because people had not been wide of the mark when they called him 'Maeldin the mad.' He had indeed, for a time, been out of his mind. He had no wish to go after new cures when the old ways were known to heal.

'Well, Maeldin,' said Merlin, 'your question is too important to be answered with mere opinion. Let us put Byzantium's wisdom to the test, follow wisdom's call to turn and see, that we may discover for ourselves and for others how the old wisdom fares beside the new, and the new in the light of the old. I suggest you continue to tend the Manstone Spring, but also partake with us of the mysteries of the Name, and we shall together discover, with the help of Taliesin, how the wisdom of Byzantium informs the Matter of Britain.'

'As to the Grail,' Merlin continued, 'there are mysteries here which cannot be discerned merely with the help of an old man's memories of caves or isles, or what he might or might not have done with the Grail. I suggest we enquire in these isles and overseas, and here beneath the tors, so that together we may discover and confirm the wisdom at their heart.'

The companions returned to their cells, pondering the mysteries of wisdom and the Name, hidden in the breath of the quartzite dragon, among the screes of Manstone Mynd.

# 3

## MAN STONE'S WISDOM DANCE

Taliesin, on his journey to Byzantium, had heard of a kingdom in the east, whose priest-king was also a prophet, like Merlin, and who was said to be a Guardian of the Holy Grail. Some months after Taliesin's return, Merlin rang the bell of Camelot and called together the community of solitary companions. Their round cells were not far apart, for each lived alone within the encircling palisade, as well as with the support of the others. So it was not every day that the companions were summoned to a gathering.

In the golden days of King Arthur, Merlin had often attended the gathering of Knights, seated at the Round Table, where each knight had his place. The Seat Perilous, which some called the seat of Judas, Merlin had reserved for the holiest of knights, owing to the fact that it was a seat of great danger. Galahad alone had eventually taken that place without betrayal, but not without great cost.

Here in the wisdom cell there was no such seat, because there was only one seat all the way round, one unbroken throne. All those who were seated together here were responsible for due regard for peril, and each upheld and encouraged the others, so that none faced peril of betrayal alone.

Merlin went to his place and sat with legs entwined, his hands at his sides. He had been pondering all that Taliesin had shared with them earlier that year. He had been wandering among the tors and had sat at the feet of the Man Stone himself, Stone King of Manstone Mynd.

In the half light of dusk, Merlin saw the Man within the Stone stir and then move, slowly at first, then faster in a kind of stately dance, chanting as he danced. What happened then, he would now share with Ganieda and Taliesin, Nimue and Dindrane, because Maeldin already knew of the Man Stone dance, for his madness was nothing of the sort, but an awakening to the language of the stones.

'The Man Stone of Manstone Mynd has stirred,' said Merlin. 'The King of the Mynd has stirred and danced.'

There was silence, except for the gentle crackle of the fire, and the sound of rain on the roof.

'The Man in the Stone came forth and danced, and in his kingly, priestly dance, he began to chant, and his chant told of his heart, turned long ago to stone, over and over again. Once was when the angels lost insight and elders became few and far between. Once was when wisdom was exiled from the Temple in Jerusalem. That was when the Book of Enoch was rejected, burned by the priests. Once was when Heraclitus became alarmed that the people of Greece were forsaking wisdom, leaving him with no alternative but to commit wisdom to writing. Before that, wisdom had been unveiled by word of mouth, passed on from heart to heart, as it was among Druid seers. Times were shallow, and the wisdom transmission of an awakened heart was increasingly despised.'

Merlin paused, but none spoke.

'It has long seemed to me that the Man Stone is a royal Sage whose wisdom is attuned to wisdom everywhere,' he continued. 'So when wisdom was neglected, as when the priests drove her from the Temple, or when wisdom was despised, rejected by men, the Man Stone froze and turned to stone. But when times are uncertain and terror threatens, and wisdom is sorely needed, the Man in the Stone unfreezes. The King of the Mynd drums and thrums his wisdom dance. In his dance, he chants, and if there is someone with a listening heart, his chant will prophesy. It is this prophecy that I have heard, and Maeldin has heard it too.'

Maeldin nodded, and his eyes were twinkling, for now he was far from madness, or else his so-called madness was his right mind.

'The Wise King's chant,' said Merlin, 'says wisdom will return, when there is a dwelling place for her to dwell in.'

Merlin paused, as if to let his words reach his heart, as well as theirs, renew vision and so begin anew. Merlin began slowly to explain.

'Some say wisdom dwells in Sarras, beyond Carbonek, Castle of the Hallows, which the British claim means Fort of the Peaks, and Bretons, Citadel of the Raven. But Sarras is anywhere and everywhere that wisdom makes her dwelling place. While many think it is somewhere in the west, I have found it in the midst. Some say there is a Grail King in India, whose function is to renew transmission of wisdom in the east, as priest-kings once did here. There is one who recently returned from India and who has news of the Grail King there, and who brings gifts from him. But that is not all.'

'In these Isles,' said Merlin, 'Arimatheans say Avalon will be unveiled again, this time inspired by wisdom's revelation of the Name. The Grail will be found again, not just in the Castle of the Grail, but anywhere where wisdom finds a dwelling place, anywhere where hearts are temples, sanctuaries of the Grail, and wisdom is welcomed home. It is this that makes the Man in the Stone drum, for his chant is the dance of wisdom.'

Merlin gazed into the wisdom dome as the flames cast dancing shadows in the heights.

'I saw the Man in the Stone dance again at dawn last week,' said Merlin. 'He did not speak, but encircled the Lion by way of the Diamond and the Eye at the head of the Throne.'

Merlin paused, and then went on.

'Recently, it came to me that a Knight of the Round Table will arrive here soon, bringing gifts from a Priest-King of the

Grail, Prester John by name. This Priest-King rules the Mar Thoma Kingdoms in India. The Knight knows Percival, your brother, Dindrane, and he seeks to meet you too, Nimue, since both of you are servants of the Holy Grail. Both of you have already opened your hearts to wisdom, so that in you both, wisdom has found her dwelling place.'

Dindrane looked at Nimue and smiled. Nimue beamed, for she knew this was a great blessing. The hidden work of a lifetime was falling into place. For Dindrane, not only was this the destiny for which she had given her life-blood once before, but it could be the fulfilment of her brother's quest, and all quests for the Grail, the uncovering of the Secret of the Grail for which Percival had fought and suffered too.

'What is his name, and from where does this Knight of the Round Table come all this way to see us?' asked Nimue.

'His name is Sir Palamedes,' said Merlin, 'and he is Duke of Provence.'

# 4

## GIFTS OF PRESTER JOHN

Sir Palamedes arrived alone on an autumn evening at dusk. His horse, tended by Maeldin, was tethered at the gate. Three geese announced his arrival, and thanks to their cackles, Ganieda heard him coming and called out to the others. Merlin hastened to greet the Knight, whom he had not seen since the year of Arthur's mortal wound. Unpacking his saddlebags, Palamedes joined them in the central round house, shared by all, where a great fire was lit, tended by whoever was cooking that day.

When all had eaten, Palamedes presented gifts of icon shrines, carved by craftsmen in the Kingdom of Mar Thoma. They were finely fashioned at the behest of India's Priest-King, Prester John, a name passed down from king to king, from generation to generation. Palamedes also brought an old scroll containing the Song of the Pearl, the story of a spiritual quest. It reminded Palamedes of the quest tales they used to hear in the Court of King Arthur, at the round table in Camelot.

Palamedes turned to Dindrane and addressed her.

'Percival, your brother, found the Grail, and now dwells in its light. For him, the quest is over, but not the light. Quests make heroes, and heroes will always need to quest, but when they grow into the light that awakened them, they begin to enter the glory whose light never ends. I learned there the Secret of the Grail, in the Court of the Grail King, Prester John. His gift of icon shrines comes with this Gift of Gifts, the Secret of the Grail.'

Taliesin, silent, listened to the flame, and Maeldin added a log to the fire in their midst.

Merlin sat deep in thought, or was it in the space between thoughts, or the clarity beyond thought, where everything arises? Pondering, Merlin began to speak.

'The Grail was sought and sometimes made a hero of the seeker, but once the Grail was found, its costly emptiness could be a shock. Some, recoiling, went in search of other quests, anything to distract them from the void. Few discerned the Secret of the Grail, as it was unveiled in the hidden heart of Joseph himself, or in the love that inspired him to offer his tomb and his shroud, the love that inspired his tenderness as he held the chalice, to embrace the blood poured forth from bleeding wounds.'

'There is a love that does not seek its own,' said Merlin. 'There is a love that lays down life for another, for others, or for all. In its light, all quests are fulfilled. All quests are complete. The Grail is found.'

Taliesin, nodding in assent, turned to Nimue and Dindrane, who responded.

'You speak of the Gift of Gifts, Sir Palamedes, and of the Secret of the Grail. What, then, of the question that forks in two? 'Who serves the Grail?' and 'Whom does the Grail serve?'

'My brother found, to his great cost and others' suffering, that this question of questions was crucial to the completion of the quest. In the end, the question emptied him of himself, so that he became the Grail that was seeking him. For him, the Secret of the Grail is that it disappears when the seeker disappears, giving way to revelation of the Grail as seeing seer and seen, the mystery of the Three. The seeing unveils the Grail right here as seer, seen in the midst.'

Palamedes remained silent, wondering how to answer Dindrane's question, or questions: 'Who serves the Grail?' and 'Whom does the Grail serve?'

It was Nimue who spoke, addressing Palamedes.

'So the Secret of the Grail is that it is most itself when it is no more. It is like the glory of a death that overcomes death once and for all.'

Suddenly, Palamedes was reminded of the moment of unveiling in the Great Cave of Hala in the Discurides. He had visited the Socotrian Isles, after he had left India and was drawing near to Arabia.

'As you all know,' Palamedes continued, 'I was the only Arabian Knight at Arthur's Court, and suffered terribly from my love for Isolde, who loved Tristan. This wound of love pierced my heart and taught me many secrets. I was sorely bruised during the Battle of Camlann, and took many months to heal.'

'When I was recovered, I travelled to Byzantium and there met a merchant from Alexandria, who was rich and influential. His name was Cosmas the Voyager, and he had been many times to India. Justinian, the Emperor of Byzantium, had given him letters to dignitaries in India, so I set sail with him to Axum, Ethiopia, and the Discurides, whose Socotrian peoples revered Mar Thoma as their Apostle. From there, we sailed to India, where we visited kingdoms in the north and south, which also revered Mar Thoma, Thomas Didymus. He had come long ago from Edessa, at the insistence of the Apostles, to be the Apostle of Socotria and India.'

'It was Cosmas who introduced me to the Priest-King of the Indian Kingdom, Prester John, who was known to be a Guardian of the Holy Grail. It was he who imparted to me the Grail Secret, transmitting it in wisdom through the Name.'

Palamades paused, and turned to Merlin, explaining the heart of the matter as best he could.

'It was off the Arabian coast of the Indian Ocean, in the Isles of the Discurides,' he said, 'that I awoke to the wisdom of the Name, and saw deeply into the Secret of the Grail. We had sailed there from Malabar by way of Taprobane, an isle of great beauty to the south of India. When we disembarked in the Discurides, we were invited to enter the Great Cave of Hala, which the Socotrians revered. Merchants had for centuries left inscriptions there, in Sanskrit, Arabic, Ethiopian, Greek, Bactrian, Tamil and Palmyran. The cavern was vast and dark, but lamps revealed crystals and treasures impossible to count.'

'I stayed behind,' continued Palamedes, 'and there awoke to what Prester John had said of the Grail, and I was seized suddenly by vision of the Name which wisdom transmits. Words too wondrous to be spoken aloud were heard in my heart, words that cannot be uttered in ordinary speech. There, in the Caverns of Hala, I saw light in whose light glory is seen in glory. I saw the timeless glory of the age to come. I entered the Holy of Holies. I awoke to the Secret of the Grail.'

'Did you ask the questions?' said Dindrane. 'Did you receive an answer to both questions among the crystals of Hala?'

Dindrane knew that first time round, Percival, her brother, had failed in this regard, but not the second. In her own case, the love she felt for Percival had somehow asked and answered both questions but she knew not how. The questions were still nagging at her heart and would not go away. Turning to Palamedes, the Saracen knight who was her brother's friend, Dindrane asked him the twin questions that seized her heart.

'Who serves the Grail? Whom does the Grail serve?'

Without hesitation, Palamedes answered her.

'Nothing serves the Grail except an illumined heart. It is the light that serves the Grail.'

Palamedes paused.

'The Grail serves nothing but the glory to come, the glory that comes from above, the glory that descends when light ascends. It is glory the Grail serves.'

Dindrane was silent, thoughtful, wondering.

Nimue, alert and attentive, sprung forward, laughing.

'It is as Merlin was saying to us,' she said. 'The Grail is an illumined heart, and the Grail serves the descent that answers ascent, glory that answers the light of an illumined heart.'

Nimue, whose discernment cut to the core, laughed from the heart. Watching her, Merlin thought that if the Grail could laugh, surely this was it. What joy to have these friends with him, here in Goatshaw Ring, on the heights of Manstone Mynd.

Taliesin, familiar with Druid seers, the prophets and priest-kings of henges and barrows in the Age of Iron, enquired of Palamedes whether the priest-kings of India knew from whence their wisdom lineage was derived.

'Through King Gundaphorus,' said Palamedes, 'and his brother, Gad, in India's northern kingdom, and Tertia, Queen in the south. Tertia was wife of King Misdaeus, who received the wisdom imparted by Mar Thoma, Apostle of India. Mar Thoma transmitted it directly from heart to heart, just as Yeshuah, his spiritual twin, transmitted it to him. He also wrote a Gospel, which was buried in a desert cave, lost for many centuries, and there are tales of him in another book, called Acts of Thomas. I have brought with me a manuscript of the oldest part, which is entitled Song of the Pearl.'

Taliesin nodded, dumbstruck and in awe, amazed that such things were known in far-off lands, and not confined to the Druid world he knew so well. The peoples of the Healing Henge had prophets and priest-kings. The elders of the Elder Days, whose barrows lie on many ancient hills, had been prophets, priests and kings, each in their domain and time.

He was astonished that in these barbarous and violent times, when Briton and Saxon were at war, and both were at the mercy of marauding Scots and Picts, Merlin had given birth to Arthur's golden age. Now that it had been and gone, here was Merlin, in touch still with mysteries of Grail Kings, transmitting their timeless wisdom for blessed times to come.

Palamedes explained to them that the wisdom of Mar Thoma had been transmitted by Yeshuah, his twin, which is why they called him Judas Thomas and Judas Didymus, which both mean Judas Twin. The wisdom of Mar Thoma's twin was none other than the wisdom of Enoch and the Son of Man. It was the wisdom of the prophets and anointed kings, transmitted through Solomon and Davidic Kings of Old Jerusalem. It was the wisdom of the Priest-King of Salem, Melchizedek, handed down before wisdom's exile from the Holy Land. The Grail Kings of India were heirs, through Mar Thoma, to the wisdom of both spiritual twins. Their wisdom was inseparable from the wisdom of the Fisher King.

The icon shrines of Prester John still adorn the wisdom cell at Goatshaw Ring, even to this day, and the Secret of the Grail, transmitted through Palamedes under Wolfstone Tor, was embraced by Merlin, and celebrated by Taliesin in his wisdom songs. Dindrane was inspired by the love in Joseph's heart, the fire that illumined the hearts of Arimatheans. Her life was permeated by twin questions: 'Who serves the Grail?' and 'Whom does the Grail serve?'

Nimue took to heart the light that serves the Grail, and the glory the Grail serves. Maeldin found that for him, the Grail Secret was none other than the living spring that brought him healing here. For Taliesin, the light in Merlin's heart mirrored the glory that the Grail serves, giving him all that he needed to renew the myth, beneath the Pendragon Tors of Manstone Mynd.

# 5

# SONG OF THE PEARL

Among the gifts brought by Sir Palamedes to Merlin was a manuscript scroll of the Song of the Pearl. In the weeks since Palamedes had departed, each of Merlin's companions read it, one by one, and pondered the mysteries it enshrined. Last of all, it was the turn of Nimue to read it, and she read it many times.

It told of a Prince of Edessa, who in the days of Parthian kings, lived as a child in the glory of his Father's Kingdom. When the time came for him to leave home, he was sent down into Egypt to bring back a precious pearl guarded by a dragon, submerged in the deeps of the sea. He was stripped of his robe of glory and went down into Egypt. There he found an inn, near to the waters where the dragon dwelt, and met a friend, a lad from his home country, and told him why he had been sent.

The Prince settled down, wore Egyptian clothes and ate Egyptian food. He fell into a kind of sleep, and completely forgot he was the son of kings and that he served the glory of his Father's Kingdom. In his profound slumber, he forgot the pearl and the quest, and lost all memory of why he was there.

Then, hearing what had befallen him, the kings and princes of Parthia wrote him a letter, reminding him of the pearl and the holiness of his quest. The letter awoke his heart from its heavy sleep, and he was illumined. He realized the bondage into which he had fallen, the slavery that had overtaken him in Egypt. When he remembered the pearl, he remembered the robe of glory that had been his. He remembered the name by which he was known and which was inscribed in the Book of Life, which is the book of those who inherit the Kingdom of Glory.

The letter flew to him like an eagle from great heights. It spoke to him like a voice unsealed from the past, reminding him of what was written in his heart. He remembered the pearl and began to enchant the dragon, charming it to sleep by the power of the Name. When the right moment came, he seized the pearl, and the garment of forgetfulness fell from him.

Returning towards the light of his Father's Kingdom, the letter became a woman's voice guiding him home. She soothed his fears and inspired his love. With her help, he rediscovered the robe of glory, the garment of light that mirrored the glory of who he really was. The robe was adorned with precious stones, each of which was an image of the King of Kings. The robe began to sing and its song raised him by its light. It restored him to his Father's glory, where he dwelt without end in his Father's Kingdom.

Nimue realized the Song of the Pearl was inspired by the wisdom of Mar Thoma and his spiritual twin, and was struck by its childlike yet profound simplicity, just like the wisdom tales of Avalon. She was not surprised that it reminded Palamedes of the tales of Camelot, for it told of a quest thwarted by oblivious forgetting, righted by wisdom in the end.

It seemed to Nimue that the strength of the tale lay in the vivid imagery of the first part of the quest, but its telling of the completion was thin.  It was heroic song, not a song of completeness, and she began to wonder how a complete wisdom song would end, or whether glory was beyond the scope of bards.

Why, she pondered, had this gift of a quest song been given to them, and what was it sent to impart?  If Mar Thoma was its original inspiration, what was his specific gift to her?  Did it throw light on the Secret of the Grail or was it to do with the Throne Mysteries of Manstone Mynd?  Was the pearl a kind of Grail, or the Grail a precious pearl?  Was the robe a key to the glory or the glory a kind of robe?  Was the letter like the questions: 'Who serves the Grail?' or 'Whom does the Grail serve?' awakening remembrance?  Was the woman actually wisdom, whose voice leads us home?

Nimue pondered all these things in her heart as she wandered over the hill.  The priceless pearl stayed with her and questioned her, like an urgent letter from wisdom.  It became her question, so that she became the pearl and was invested with the robe of glory too.

The landscape spoke of lightning drawn to quartz, but the inscape unveiled lightning in the quartz, cutting its way to the

Throne. The inscape gave Nimue direct insight beyond concepts, opening the eye of her heart. The tors became a hallowed place of disclosure, where her pearl and its glory were unveiled as bright quartz in dark tors. Here was wisdom's dwelling place, her Sarras, veiled yet unveiled among black dragon tors on Manstone Mynd.

# 6

## EYE OF THE NEEDLE

Nothing brought greater joy to the companions on the hill than to witness Merlin and Nimue renewing the wisdom of the elders, and Taliesin restoring the sacred tradition of the bards. Their work was sustained by the love and wisdom of Ganieda, Maeldin and Dindrane, who absorbed what they received, and reflected it back to them again. Each was the mirror of the others, and the others a mirror to each, a spontaneous co-inherence that was wondrous to behold.

Most days, Nimue would wander the length of Manstone Mynd, from the Wolfstone, where shepherds of wisdom gathered, to Lionstone Tor, where the cranberries grew. Often Merlin would be gone for hours at a time, and sometimes for days. Nimue would see him seated in deep quiet on the Throne, always entering by way of the Needle's Eye, a mysterious opening in the great rock just southwest of the Throne.

The Eye of the Needle was an ancient door of initiation, formed by a huge fragment of fallen rock creating a passage between towering crags of the Throne, like a window between worlds. A great slab of stone was jammed at an angle over the gap between two tors, creating a natural arch, which looked from beneath like a bright eye, gleaming out of the rock.

It had long been Merlin's practice to climb the Throne, which faced northeast, by way of the Eye of the Needle. This passage between worlds led him to the Throne by going right round it, and then into it, uniting him to its central axis, above and below. Without the Needle's Eye, which awoke the eye of his heart, the Throne would be just another crag, and not even the highest at that, because Manstone Tor was higher.

Nimue, too, would pass through the Eye of the Needle to the Throne, always alone, when Merlin was at home in his cell, for Merlin had initiated her into its mysteries, as well as those of Lionstone Tor. This was a quartzite crag that looked from both sides like a monstrous lion, gazing southwest over the slopes where the cranberries grew. The Lion's glare reigned over Nipstone Rock and Black Rhadley Hill. Between the Lionstone and the Manstone tors lay the Diamond Rock, which Nimue knew opened to the mysteries of the Lion. Each pinnacle had its energies, its sacred names and powers, and Nimue was now familiar with them all.

The Diamond Rock to the south was key to the secrets of the Lion, as the Needle's Eye was to the Throne of the Man Stone King. It cut through all that obscured the wisdom of the Lion, just as the Needle dissolved all that hindered access to the Man enthroned. The wise master of them all was the Man Stone himself, who stood to the north of the tor that bore his name, towering over the forest wilderness like a King. The Man in the Stone never revealed his wisdom to any who had not submitted to the diamond-cutting clarity of the Diamond Stone, without which the wisdom of the Lion remained hidden too. How the Lion related to the Man was something Nimue was working on, for it held many keys to the mysteries of the Throne.

Sometimes the tors looked like castle ruins, abandoned long ago. Sometimes they appeared to be the hardened spine of an enormous dragon, whose sleeping grandeur threatened to awaken and devour all in sight. Scarred screes of jagged stones serrated the slopes like dragon scales. Sometimes, Nimue saw the tors as guardians of the forest, black quartzite kings whose castles needed no defence, for they were impregnable. They might look ruined, but they retained all their power, as Nimue discovered as she learned their mysterious ways.

Agravain, like Morgana, named the Throne the Devil's Chair. Mordred also called it that when he had studied the darker powers, only to be overpowered by them. Nimue knew that to assume power over subtle powers was dangerous, because it gave them power, power to overpower the unsuspecting pride hidden at the core of presumption. Morgana had made that mistake, and the powers had taken their toll. Using Mordred, they had broken the union of the Round Table and torn the land apart.

Nimue still loved those who had been caught up in this torment, and she hoped to find ways to undo what had been done. She knew Morgana was a true fay, and that it was fay powers and not Morgana or Mordred that were behind the catastrophe of Camlann. Indeed, Morgana was a Lady of the Lake, and that was

Nimue's destiny too. Here the stones held secrets that transmitted wisdom old and new, capable of renewing the world. That is why Nimue sought out Merlin and joined him in this sanctuary, to uncover the wisdom crying out from quartzite stones, wisdom longing to be loved and known.

Beneath the tors, from Roman times, generations of miners had dug for lead and other minerals, leaving old workings that delved far down into the deeps. Nimue knew of old stairways into the shafts and caves that led to other times, and sometimes, to other worlds. She had discovered Merlin's crystal cave, and studied the secrets of the inner quartz. There were fires down there that only Merlin knew, but Nimue, aware of her limits, did not cross the sacred bounds.

Openings to other worlds did not frighten her, but if she were going to help undo what had gone wrong, she would need to know the ways of light. She had long known that although quartz looked black on the hill, it was in fact white crystal, translucent to the eye, bright and sparkling. The dark tors above hid glistening worlds beneath, luminous and illumining.

There was no end to the light in the quartz or to vision in crystal stones. There was no end to the glory of stars in stones, for it was everywhere. Forests now grew where ice had been, but the tors had always soared above both, with light within. The light held the key, even if the glory could never, like a mine, be exhausted.

Nimue knew her limits, but Merlin was passing on to her the wisdom of the Nine, which was her destiny. He saw deeply into the mysteries of the Lake, which were the secrets of deep remembrance. He also knew the secrets of the nine rings, which had been lost when wisdom withdrew, and found again when she returned. Rings of power were originally rings of wisdom, rings of light that purified and illumined their bearers. But if the bearer let darkness in, power might corrupt, so Nimue sought to learn the ways of light.

Ganieda was content to attend to the roots required if the wisdom work of Merlin was to be safely earthed. The elemental energies were strong and things could get out of balance. Dindrane worked with the questions of the Grail, and so it was the love of the Arimatheans that sustained her. Maeldin cut logs in the woods, fetched water and tended the garden by the desert cells. He was attentive to the wisdom of the healing spring. He was often out on the hill, and kept an eye out for Merlin when he was on his own. He did not interfere, but was attentive to the needs of the elder, in case he might have need of him.

The heart of Merlin's work was the mystery of the Throne. It was an axis that passed through the midst of all worlds, so it was where he abode, day by day, even when he was at peace in his cell. The Throne called for the Needle's Eye, because the Eye undid all that interferes with the Throne. No hindrance could overpower the Needle's Eye. It severed what confused and what divided it made one.

Merlin always entered by way of the Eye, and never forced his own way in, which would let the powers in too, so the powers had nothing to grasp. There was nothing to give them a grip. The Throne could ascend, the Throne might descend, but the powers found no way in.

Merlin was already familiar with the seven realms, as above, so below. But when Taliesin returned from Byzantium, he had been able to throw fresh light on how the realms above were connected with the realms below. When Palamedes had visited them with gifts from India, Merlin had immediately been drawn to what Palamedes had called the Gift of Gifts, the Secret of the Grail. He had taken this to heart and brought it to the Throne.

As Merlin strengthened links with what was above, so he was able to embrace what was below. Here, wisdom became the embrace of stones below in the strength of stars above. She revealed the mysteries of Lionstone Tor. The strength above was essential to the embrace of what was below. The Throne required the strength of the Lion, if the wisdom of the Man were to ascend and descend the Throne.

It was not Merlin by himself, or in his own power, who worked this great work. It was the wisdom of the Man, which prophets and seers in Byzantium called the wisdom of the Son of Man, who worked this royal work. Byzantium was heir, in this regard, to Enoch, the Prophet-Seer, who knew the older wisdom of the Temple in Jerusalem, before she was driven out. Elders knew of the Throne in elder days, but Merlin was aware not only of the Throne here on the hill, but of Enoch too.

The elders of the Healing Henge and Barrow tombs had studied the secret language of the stones, and knew that there was correspondence between what was above and what was below. Enoch showed that the Son of Man must be all that he sees, if he is to ascend and descend with the Throne. This gave Merlin insight into the renewing mysteries of the Needle's Eye and Throne.

Enoch not only showed how to ascend and descend, but unveiled himself as the Man in the Stone, only to disappear in favour of another, the Son of Man, Mar Thoma's spiritual twin. Merlin discovered his name, *Yeshuah*, but also that this name *Yah Shuah* enshrined the Name of names, *Yah*, which Enoch knew. The Throne enthroned this very Name of names, as Taliesin discovered in Byzantium. It was the heart of his Song of the Name.

Merlin spent many years at work with the Man in the Stone. He explored the ramifications of the Needle's Eye, and circled round into the Throne, delving down into the depths beneath. He ascended above in order to descend below, always along the central axis of the Throne. The mysteries he unveiled there were beyond his powers of expression, but he was able to share with Nimue the practice of turning and the vision of seeing that worked the holy work.

The fruits of this spiritual work were shared with their companions, day by day, as wisdom was kneaded into the loaf, like leaven in the lump. Each of them lived wisdom as their own, yet partook of it as the life they shared. All in all, there was nothing left out that was not renewed by the Man in the Stone, King on the Throne. Nothing was shut out, not even Mordred or Morgana, Briton or Saxon, Scot or Pict.

Taliesin was fond of the wisdom round cell, where he could practise poetry and chant alone by the fire. He had been the king's poet, in Camelot. Before that, he had been a bard of brave princes, like Brochwel in Powys, and Urien Rheged in Strathclyde.

Now Taliesin was old, and the journey to the east had tired him, but it had not quenched his song. He did not need Merlin to tell him what he was doing on the hill. He already knew, and he was busy turning poetry into prophecy, and shaping it as chant.

Taliesin was aware of Nimue, too, and although he was not often on the hill, as Maeldin was, he was attentive to her presence, and caring too. He was the voice of the Throne, as he had been the voice of Arthur's throne in golden days now past, and of the woe that befell them all, when Mordred had usurped the king.

Now, he sang of Man and Stone, King and Throne, of vision and of light, inklings of glory half-remembered, hints of glory still to come. But what song might embrace deadly foes, Pict and

Briton, Saxon and Scot? What song might still the hatred of warring tribes and embrace them all? Could wisdom chant heal broken hearts, and free fallen powers to be what they were meant to be? Was wisdom able to discern the Secret of the Grail?

'Who serves the Grail? Light illumining the heart,' he sang. 'Whom does the Grail serve? Glory unveiling a Kingdom come, healing the land.'

Taliesin the bard retold the myth to restore the Throne. The wisdom transmission of Merlin the Sage wedded stars and stones in dazzling quartz, on the slopes of Manstone Mynd.

# 7

# TALIESIN BENEATH WOLFSTONE TOR

To the east of Wolfstone Tor, where the wisdom shepherds used to meet, there was a hollow known as Fissure Fold, where surrounding slopes converged.  At its centre, there was a ravine that led down into ancient fissures beneath the Throne.  Perhaps melting ice had gouged out caverns there, or perhaps it was the work of miners from Viroconium in Roman times, searching for lead and silver.

Seers would meet here, in times of crisis, and Taliesin remembered a gathering of kings from the north, at which bards were consulted and their prophecies heard.  He had known Urien Rheged, leader of the Britons in the north, and Rhydderch of Cumbria, Ganieda's royal spouse, and most of the British princes of the north.

Now that Taliesin was old, he was at peace here, for like Merlin he had come south to escape the ravages of war.  As a young bard, he had been poet for a time in the household of young Brochwel of Pengwern.  Here, the Cornovians still protected the forest wildwoods to the west of Caer Guricon, which Roman Britons called Viroconium, white city of the woods. Brochwel's father, Cyngen the Renowned, had commanded here a remnant of Roman knights of Britain, and ruled the region of

Pengwern. He was called Aurelius Caninus, denounced by Gildas, but wedded to Tudlwysti, patron of saints. The Pengwern Cornovians refortified the old citadel on the Wrekin and rebuilt Viroconium, using new timber over old stones of Rome.

The British held firm here in Pengwern, but probably not for long, for the Mercians were pushing west to confine them to the western hills. The lands of the river Gwern, or Severn, were safe for a while, defended by trained cavalry with scarlet cloaks, like Arthur's Red Dragon knights. But Taliesin had been witness to an irrevocable defeat in the north, and his fellow bards had mourned the loss of countless kings.

The British were losing the battle for Britain. Gildas might be inspiring a new generation to rebuild their lives in monasteries, but the golden days of Arthur's Britain were gone.

Taliesin was inspiring bards to reinterpret the Matter of Britain to include the English, so that the Saxon conqueror in Mercia might be persuaded to adopt the sacred culture of conquered Britain.

It was the task of the bards to retell the legends of Arthur's Britain for the English, to make Saxon as well as Briton heir to Merlin's wisdom. Here, on Manstone Mynd, seer and bard had joined, bequeathing to Britain a vision of a once and future golden time, an age where wisdom would be loved and known again.

Arthur's Britain was no more, but Merlin's Britain lived on in the wisdom song of Taliesin and the bards. Disaster bears witness to glory, and division to unity, a united Britain, a kingdom rooted in kindness and wisdom. The legacy of Roman Britain might now extend to embrace Angle and Pict, Jute and Scot, or else be forever forgotten. Merlin's conquest of the English by Britain was to be a victory of wisdom, not of war, and defeated Britons would transmit glory in defeat, and embrace foe as friend in wisdom's Name.

Taliesin would sometimes return to Fissure Fold in Wolfstone Hollow and ponder the defeats in the north. Like Merlin, war had deranged his mind for a time, but here on Manstone Mynd, healing song was working its gentle remedies. Companions with broken hearts were tending each other's wounds, and in the caves beneath the Throne, wounds were beginning to heal, creating times and worlds anew.

The Matter of Britain, in Taliesin's hands, would deepen to include the English, too, and so unite warring factions in a wise embrace. His task was to make the poetic 'making' true, able to come true again and again, in age after age. He needed Merlin's wisdom for this, and Nimue's insight into the Lake. He needed Ganieda's steadiness and Dindrane's unselfish love. Maeldin's healing, like his, was not a private affair, but one with the healing of the land. For the bard, such healing meant a hallowing of hallows and the myth. It meant tales were being retold in better ways, mirroring a completeness that only wisdom knows.

When Taliesin descended into the depths beneath the Throne, he was witness to the Throne's wooing of warring powers, to heal the ills of wounds. To descend beneath the Throne meant, for Taliesin, braving the powers in the deepest delves, wresting the pearl from their grasp, and reclaiming the glory that was lost. The Song of the Pearl meant the poet heeds the prophetic reminder and fulfils his call. It meant restoring light from light and welcoming glory home.

Taliesin read Mar Thoma's Song of the Pearl in the light of the Song of the Name. The Name sends powers to sleep, so that the dragon fails to notice when the pearl is gone. The Prince returns to the kingdom of light with the pearl, to renew transmission of glory from seer to seer.

The form of the Grail as such is not the point. The pearl is the light that serves the Grail, and the robe is the glory the Grail serves.

Taliesin's wound would be healed when the wound of the Fisher King was healed, and that would be the healing of the land. Wisdom was pouring forth from delved deeps beneath the Throne, enlightening the world. The light of quartzite tors wedded the glory of stars in stones, on silver slopes of Manstone Mynd.

# 8

# THRONE VISION

The Great Tor of the Throne was Merlin's axial point, at once a place in space and timeless presence in the midst. For him, Throne vision was his spiritual work every day. It was the wisdom that inspired his life. He would ascend the hill and encircle the tors, always remembering to pass through the Eye of the Needle, for the broken tor was an open door to the Throne. There he was unburdened of all hindrance that encumbered him, and went round to where old steps ascend the Throne. He sat to one side, leaving the Chair alone, open to heaven.

Recently, the Throne had not been empty. To the eye of his heart, the sovereign's seat was filled, but not by someone he could clearly see. At first, it seemed to be Enoch, then the Son of Man that Enoch saw, in radiant form divine. The figure of wisdom he had seen to the north of Manstone Tor was the Man in the Stone, seated here on the Throne.

Merlin knew it was the Man, although he had not seen him come. Recently, back at the tor, he had seen him move, drum and thrum his stately dance, but that was all. Yet somehow he knew it was the Man in person as the Stone, enthroned here in the midst of stars, alone, yet not alone.

Merlin, trembling, was overawed, struck dumb by wonder, silent, as the Man's gaze saw through him to seeing that was not sight; rather, Merlin saw he was being seen. Throne vision was not just sight of something. You became what you saw, seeing as you were seen, just as Enoch became the Son of Man he saw. Merlin knew that it was not a matter of sight but of turned insight, and he trusted what he saw. He became what seeing sees, the seer that is all that wisdom sees.

When the Throne began to ascend, Merlin ascended too and entered a sanctuary, transparent like crystal, in which all worlds inhered and all times were present, simultaneous, and whole. When, again, the Throne ascended, so did the Man, and Merlin too, as tongues of fire, beyond translucence. He entered through a living flame into a further place, an inmost sanctuary awesome to behold. The Holy of Holies was empty, filled with glory, which embraced him.

Enoch was with him; or rather he now seemed to be Enoch, for he saw with another's eye, purer than his own. This place was not a confined space, but opened everywhere, all light, all flame. Rivers flowed from beneath the Throne, light so glorious that he had to avert his gaze.

The Man was there, enthroned, his gaze so radiant that none could look on him. This was the Man in the Stone, but arrayed as he is, on the Throne. The stone to the north of Manstone Tor was none other than this Man, the Man in the Stone, King on his Throne, embracing all times and worlds.

Then Merlin saw, or maybe Enoch saw, that as the Throne ascended, so it was simultaneously descending on its own axis, still at centre, heart of all times and worlds. As the Throne ascended, it embraced the Lion, the Lion of Lionstone Tor. As it descended, it was the body of the dragon, whose serrated spine was a line of jagged tors, whose scales clad slopes in pairs. As the body of the dragon, land and Throne were one; landscape and inscape were a single weave. The dragon was flaming energy, ablaze as quartzite light in the midst of Manstone Mynd.

Merlin discerned that the Throne was gathering to itself all souls, all spirits, embracing and ascending with them to fair sanctuaries above. He saw with Enoch's eye that, for the Throne above, these hells were heavens, and that all those who were saying 'yes' were present here in heavens above.

Those who were saying 'no' were not yet here, but the Throne was nonetheless embracing and welcoming them, never forcing them. They were free to awaken above, as soon as they were ready to say 'yes.' The hells could not hold them, for hells had no power unless they were given power. It was the 'no' that gave them power. It was the 'no' that turned luminous lords into lurking lucifers, and it was the 'yes' that undid their agonies. Merlin realized that this work had always been his, to tend the recalcitrant 'no,' that it might rise from 'no' to 'yes,' 'yes' to light, 'yes' to glory without end.

Then Enoch, or was it the Man, beckoned to Merlin to draw near. The old sage was in utter awe, and was quite struck dumb, as he heard a voice speak to him, telling him not to be afraid as, slow and solemn, limpid and serene, it delivered utterance:

'The powers have no hold here. Their function was to bring blessing, but they stooped and brought a curse. Their task was to watch over those entrusted to them, but they brought war and slaughter, causing confusion wherever they went. It was their betrayals that tricked Agravain, and twisted Mordred into usurping the king. Camlann was their victory, or so they claimed, but wisdom heals the land. The dragon's armour holds the keys, for each tor is a door, opening to wisdom above, bringing healing to all below.'

Merlin watched, aware that many watchers watched, in many times and many worlds. The voice spoke a Word to the watchers, each in his time and place. The Word was addressed to Enoch, but also, in him, to all who, like Merlin, were entrusted with prophecy, with the work of the seer, and with the guidance of kings. Merlin was prophet, mage and seer, witness to an axial presence, by virtue of the Throne. Throne vision was not special for him. It was the Matter of Seers, the food they eat. They breathe its air.


Merlin began to sway, as the Throne became a radiant ring. He was listening in, as dumb stones began to sing.

'Two become one as, one by one, seven hells are restored to seven heavens.

'Two are one as, one from one, births Man from Man, transmitting wisdom as she goes.

'Two make one, one through one, as Man makes Man, transformed from stone to Throne.

'Two are one, one as one, when stone and Throne, Lion and stone, shape shift, and dance as One.'

Merlin felt the old magic stirring as he swayed, and was amazed that the new wisdom was as strong as the old, and that Enoch went back to the beginning, just as the elders of the Healing Henge had done. What Enoch saw is what the elders of the Elder Days had seen, unveiling wisdom in stars and stones.

Merlin remembered that glory here was not in time, and that what appeared in time as before or after was ever present and wide aware right here. The once and future king was free now of the past, free of future too. What was and what is to come dissolve here now, because the Throne is, and always was, just as it is, the living presence of the King. This is the timeless time of Man, Man in Stone, Stone made Man.

Merlin's residual doubt, not resolved until now, melted in the swing and sway of wisdom song. Old and new, first and last, became a single dance here, when the glory moved to the drum, to the thrum and swing of the dancing Man.

Two are one here, yes indeed, as Merlin dissolved to stone, leaving a rumour that he had been turned to stone. They accused Nimue of this, ever eager to blame a woman, as if every fay seer was a wicked witch, and her magic malevolent and dense.

What they did not know was that stone turned back into Man again, so there was nobody to blame. Merlin seen was one with the Man, seeing him turn from man to stone and stone to man, two made one and one made two, over and over again.

All this was not Merlin's magic. It was never just Merlin's magic. It was the magic of Man, the man in the stone, the magic of stone unveiled in the Man. The two were one and the one was two, never easy for stone-hard hearts to understand. But this wisdom melts hearts, so they can see, this dance of two made one and one made three.

Three was revealed as a triple spiral in the wisdom of the Healing Henge, remembered by elders in the Temple on the Boyne, between Knowth and Dowth, long ago. The triple spiral was one yet two because the convex and the concave curves were one, unveiling the inner and the outer faces of one spiralling dance. One curve embraces visible worlds, and includes us all, and the other embraces invisible worlds, which look like other worlds to us. But wisdom discerns the two are one, dissolving the doubt of the stone-hard hearts in the swing and sway of the dance.

Merlin knew this triune wisdom, and was glad to discover it was alive and well in the wisdom of Byzantium. Bards could renew the wisdom of the Mage again, now that the Man in the Stone of Manstone Mynd had danced. There was no question of tearing the land apart, in the name of race or religion. The Matter of Britain was not a matter of race or religion, but of the embrace of wisdom, renewing the land from the Throne.

Merlin's legacy was not just Arthur's thirty years of peace, but a legacy of wisdom that made the two one in the mystery of three, in any and every age. This was Merlin's work, not his alone, but the work of the Throne, the work of the Man in the Stone, the work of Pendragon wisdom, with rings of light cleansing the riven rings of power.

Finger rings, wrist rings, arm rings, neck rings were all wrought by masters of fire, who mined, smelted, forged and tempered torques and bracelets, swords and crowns. Smiths and alchemists were masters of creative fires that forged heirloom rings and wedding rings, rings of patriarchs and reigning kings. Swords and crowns were Merlin's concern as well as rings of kings. The wisdom of smiths and alchemists was Merlin's care, because the ruin of Britain was due to ring wars and blood feuds between warring British kings.

Merlin knew that the Manstone mines were key to rings of power, and he was aware that Gildas sought to hallow crowns by inspiring haloed saints to hallow the rings of kings. Ring quests could no longer be driven solely by a ruthless will to power, as they were in the Age of Bronze and Iron. Power corrupted when rings of domination usurped rings of light, and refused to pass through the ring of fire that purified their energies, and freed them of a ruthless will to power.

Wisdom's work in the Manstone mines beneath the tors was forging renewed rings of power in netherworlds, rings of wisdom in rings of fire. Merlin was hallowing swords and crowns where they were mined and forged, where rings of power were purified by fire in caves of light, forging renewing rings of peace, concealed beneath Manstone Mynd.

# 9

# MINSTER IN THE WOODS

A minster lay northwest of Manstone Mynd, a monastery called Minster Ley, constructed of wattle and wood. In a clearing in the forests, called a Ley, the Rea Brook ran, watering the land. The Ley was a good place for a minster, because it provided lush pasture near to running streams, a place to grow vegetables, crops and fruit. The monastery was sheltered by the forests of Pengwern, safe in their shade, swathed in dappled light.

Teilo was the first to settle a few monks here, at the invitation of Cyngen the Renowned, who refortified Caer Guricon and the Wrekin Moot. Teilo also founded a larger minster at Llandeilo Fawr, and was Bishop in Demetia. Later, when the plague came, Teilo crossed to Brittany, New Britain over Sea, but his minster thrived in Old Britain, in the shire of west Pengwern.

These were times when many monks were inspired by Gildas, whose writings on the Ruin of Britain had encouraged Teilo and Samson to withdraw into solitude, to save what they could from the ruin of Britain, eventually creating a new Britain in Brittany. Gildas spoke warmly of Arthur's reign, but had his own reasons for not mentioning his name. He spoke bitterly of the tyranny and violence of warring British kings, and the anarchy following Arthur's demise. He spoke scathingly of the tyrant, Aurelius Caninus, although Cyngen was a generous patron of saints, as was his saintly Queen, Tudlwysti.

Gildas despaired of the ruin of Britain and his solution was monasteries. His book on the Ruin of Britain was a tremendous success. Monasteries sprang up everywhere, even in Pengwern. The young took to the hills and isles, with Gildas as their inspiration, spreading peace in place of war. Eventually Gildas retired to the realm of saints he had founded, a Britain renewed by hallowing peace, called Brittany.

One of the monks of Minster Ley, Gerontius, was a relative of Cyngen and Brochwel, rulers of Powys and Pengwern. He was fond of Maeldin, and would climb round the north tors of the Mynd to see him. He had been a disciple of Cadoc, and like him, was of the spiritual lineage of Illtud of Llanilltud Fawr. He was later ordained priest by Bishop Dubricius of Gwent, who had himself founded minsters to the south, on the banks of the River Wye. Dubricius also founded monasteries in the Archenfeld, which Roman Britons called Ariconium.

Minster Ley had never attracted more than just a few brethren. One of them, a Saxon named Wulfstan, a local man, had been elder there for many years. Some say he was named after Wolfstone Tor, the Rock of the Shepherds above Fissure Fold, and that his forebears once lived on Manstone Mynd.

Wulfstan thought well of Maeldin, but had been wary of Merlin, puzzled by the respect shown to him by those who had known Arthur. He was a stranger to the old ways of Taliesin and the bards, and knew little of Byzantium, still less of the temple wisdom of Enoch and Old Jerusalem. He strongly disapproved of women up here with Merlin, and had no understanding of Nimue and the mysteries of the Lake. Still, Merlin and his companions warmly welcomed him, and he enjoyed the hospitality of their table and their hearth.

Wulfstan had little time for the rigours of Saint David in Minervia and preferred the gentler ways of Cadoc and Gildas. David's life was strict, inspired by the desert fathers of Egypt, whereas Cadoc preferred cultured vision, perhaps reflecting royal origins. At Llancarfan, it is said he kept a hundred men at arms in a hill fort above his monastery, which gave him peace of mind. But then, he was still a king, and combined his royal duties with those of abbot. Minster Ley had the protection of the Cornovian kings, and the knights of Caer Guricon, but was not strict, reflecting the moderation of Illtud.

Gerontius had met Kentigern in the north, in his forest retreat in Caledonia. They shared a mutual affection and respect, but lost touch when Gerontius fled south to the Minster at Meifod, near the summer hunt of the kings of Powys and Pengwern. There, he met Prince Tysilio of Powys, son of Brochwel of Caer Guricon. Tysilio was taking refuge with his elder, Gwyddfarch, hiding from his royal relatives. Tysilio felt obliged to flee further afield, for Meifod was in Powys lands, so settled on the isle in the Menai Straits that bears his name, becoming one of the apostles of Anglesey. Gerontius later left Meifod to join Wulfstan at Minster Ley, and only met Tysilio again when Brochwel's son returned to be abbot of Meifod.

Tysilio, like Brochwel and Cyngen, understood the old ways, and sought to integrate all that was valid of the wisdom of the elder days. Meifod was not far from Minster Ley, so occasionally Gerontius would meet Tysilio there. When Tysilio fled to Brittany to escape being crowned King of Powys and Pengwern, Gerontius eventually lost touch with him. It was said that Melangell inspired Tysilio, for Meifod was not far from Pennant, and both were escaping royal destinies.

Again and again, Brittany was refuge to Britons for whom the ruin of Britain had become unbearable. Gildas inspired them to become monks, and Merlin, although not one of them, was in touch with many of them. They saw him as the pagan Druid who dabbled in magic to serve his king, and Taliesin as the Bard who stubbornly clung to old pagan, meaning 'country', ways. They had no inkling what Merlin and Taliesin were actually doing here, nor had they vision of the Matter of Britain, beyond the obvious symbols which their religion prescribed.

One exception was Brochwel, the Cornovian King, son of Cyngen the Renowned. He gladly gave his protection to Merlin, and to the Minster in the forest Ley over the hill. His capital, Caer Guricon, was still heir to Arthur's peace, and that included old ways as well as new. The migration of a large force of Cornovians to Cornwall in recent years, to check the Irish, had depleted their numbers, as had the departure of the Dumnonian branch to Devon. Merlin was aware that Brochwel's remaining Cornovians were perhaps Roman Britain's last stand. Pengwern under his rule was at peace, but how long this peace would last, nobody could tell.

Another exception was Caranticus, one of the monks of the Minster in the Ley, who had been a close friend of Oran, disciple of Columba of Iona. Prince of the Royal House of Tara in Ireland, Columba might have been High King of all Ireland, if he had not become a monk. Conflict over laws of copyright and of sanctuary had led Columba to terrible slaughter, at the Battle of Cudrevne, at which three thousand lives were lost. The scale of this violence outraged monasteries of the defeated High King, and at the Synod of Telltown, Columba was excommunicated. Following the intercession of Brendan of Birr, his sentence was commuted, and he was exiled from Ireland.

Caranticus knew that the trauma of war had left such deep marks on Columba that in Iona peace became his legacy. Peace was the legacy of Aidan and Columban monks on Lindisfarne, and of Columbanus' monks in Bobbio and Burgundy. Maeldin, eager to hear about the deep roots of Columban peace, sought out Caranticus at Minster Ley.

Caranticus told him that kings in Dal Riada, Pictland and Strathclyde had taken Columba's peace to heart. They refused to make war on each other as they used to do. This rejoiced Maeldin's heart, for he had himself been driven out of his mind by poisonous war, as Merlin had by its relentless savagery. Columba's renunciation of war and violence was the lasting fruit of his exile from Ireland. Caranticus knew that Merlin's deep wisdom had to do with peace, so he was prepared not to condemn his so-called magic out of hand.

The ruin of Britain, according to Gildas, had not been the work of Saxon invaders, or Irish marauders, but of the relentless violence of British kings among themselves. Gildas sought to inspire peace, not through war, as Arthur did, but through monasteries, as in Egypt Antony did. Now, in the north, Columba was inspiring peace, like Gildas, through monasteries that influenced kings. Caranticus' friend, Oran, had laid down his life to found this peace on Iona, grounding the monastery on costly love. His church, next to the monastery of Iona, was a lasting reminder of the love that lays down its life to make peace.

Caranticus would accompany Gerontius when he visited Maeldin, and Merlin would listen to them, content that peace was inspiring peace at last, even among warring Britons, Picts and Scots in Dal Riada. His heart was one with Oran on his isle, with Columba at the foot of the Throne, as he wrestled with powers that seduced men to war. In this crucible at the heart of the Throne on the Mynd, the energy of the dragon was transforming, breaking through to a spirit of peace instead of war.

Regarding the legacy of peace, a profound accord was growing between Elder Wulfstan, Gerontius and Caranticus, monks of Minster Ley, and the companions in Merlin's desert, Goatshaw Ring beneath Wolfstone Tor, on Manstone Mynd.

# 10

# DOVES FROM THE DOVE OF PEACE

Merlin was grateful to Caranticus for news of Columba's peace. But what happened next was unexpected. One of the monks of Iona, Virgno, of British descent, came south to visit Merlin, carrying a gift from Columba of Iona. In a wicker basket, strapped to his saddle, there was a flock of six white doves. Columba's name meant dove, and his love of peace found expression, now, in this gift to Arthur's Seer, a gift of doves of purity and peace.

The dove was symbol of the Holy Spirit, having been a symbol of peace in Old Europe's temples long ago. Virgno urged Merlin to build a columbarium to house Columba's gift of doves, signs of peace in an age of war. So, with Virgno's help, for he was young and strong, Maeldin built a dovecote close to the gate, and whoever came to Merlin's desert on Manstone Mynd would be reminded, on entering, of Columba's gift of peace, communicating great peace. The royal novice who had been chief among warrior princes in the west was now a prophet, mage and seer, making peace in the north.

When Caranticus heard that Virgno had come from Iona, he set out with Gerontius from Minster Ley. Virgno was delighted to see him, because he knew he had been a friend of Oran.

Several monks in Iona recently reported visions of Oran rising from the dead, saying that hell was not at all as it was said to be. The monks were disturbed by this, and were uncertain what he meant. Columba made no comment, but Eithne, Columba's mother, who was living on Hinba, an Isle of Saints in the Isles of the Sea, said that the visions were inspired. She said that when Oran gave his life's blood to found the peace of Iona, he saw deeply into the glory of unselfish love.

Amma Eithne said Oran bore witness to a profound truth, that fires of hell are fires of burning boundless love. It was this love that was the living flame of peace. It was this love that inspired their peace in the isles. It was this love that restored seven hells to sevenfold peace, a sevenfold heaven of peace on hallowed earth.

Merlin listened as Virgno told of visions of Oran in Iona, and of Eithne of the royal house, discerning their import in the Isles of the Sea. Caranticus was visibly moved, for Oran had been a beloved friend of his. Deep in his heart, he sensed the visions of Oran were true. He turned to Merlin to see what he would say. Merlin, usually reluctant to pronounce on such matters, on this occasion spoke from the heart.

'These visions are genuine prophecy and can be trusted, for they are true. Hell is divine love, not a created place. If we reject it, its fire will burn. If we accept it, its light illumines, and if it is loved and known, its glory hallows all who see. Oran's love was deep, and these visions of his vision of love are true. Love is Oran's prophecy. Love is the foundation of peace.'

Eithne had not forgotten that Columba, the name she gave her son, meant dove of peace. Peace inspired Iona's saints, and Virgno saw this gift of doves to Merlin as a gift of peace from the Dove of Peace. Merlin's heart was glad, for it confirmed the work of Throne vision, his peace-making war with wars and savage powers. The monks might not understand, but wisdom work was as crucial to them as it was to the land. It was not something weird, but the Matter of Britain, remaking the myth to renew the land.

Virgno was young, but in later years, after Baithene and Laisren, succeeded Columba as abbot of Iona. He was the youth who, from a side chapel where he had been praying, saw Columba clothed in light. Virgno was a Briton, so Columba had singled him out for this journey, because he spoke British as well as Gaelic, the language of Iona and Dal Riada.

A gift of doves reminded Nimue of doves fashioned in old stone symbols of wisdom in the days of the Hunt. It reminded her of wisdom doves carved in the sanctuaries of Sumeria, and signet seals of doves in Nineveh and Crete. The lore of Avalon was not forgetful of the doves of Knossos and the palace of Hagia Triada, the doves of the wise Lady of Carchemish and Hierapolis. Avalon was aware of the doves in Anatolian shrines of Cybele,

66

whose son, Attis, was wise shepherd of the stars. White doves were votive offerings in the temples of Mycenae, Phoenicia and Phrygia, and it was a dove at eventide that offered Noah the olive leaf that told him the floodwaters were going down.

The rainbow covenant was the gift of a dove, the peace of the dove of Ararat, bringing peace in place of war. A dove was a symbol of the Spirit at Pentecost, and doves carried the chi-rho fish on tombs in Roman catacombs. Seven doves depicted the Spirit's seven gifts in Byzantine art, and a dove was mounted on the tips of wisdom sceptres, carried by nine Ladies of the Lake in Avalon. Wisdom was Queen of Peace in many cultures, as Nimue knew, and the dove in Avalon was a messenger of peace.

Nimue had been listening attentively to Virgno, for she was well aware of the importance to Ireland of Derry, Durrow, and the Kells. She knew that Columba was to the Dal Riadan Scots what Merlin was to Arthur's Britain, prophet, mage and seer. Tales of Merlin told of the prophet, mage and seer, just as tales of Columba were to do. The cultural context differed, as Gaels were not Britons, but the lineaments of wisdom were clear.

Prophecy transmitted wisdom, renewed by the mage in moments of power, discerned by the seer, that all may turn and see. When the time eventually came for a Life of Columba to be written, Adamnan and his monks would revere him as prophet, mage and seer, just as tales of Merlin were to do.

It would seem that Columba's gift showed he was aware that Merlin was a prophet of peace, a seer of wisdom and a mage whose powers were dedicated to peace. Nimue saw that his gift brought with it not only a blessing of peace, but generous empowerment to make peace. Nimue knew of traditions connecting the dragon and the dove. She saw that Merlin's work of the Throne was making peace, and that her work, too, lay here, working the mysteries of peace, in the depths of the dragon of Manstone Mynd.

# 11

# THE WHOLE WORLD IN A RAY OF SUN

Merlin's companions invited Virgno to stay for a few days on Manstone Mynd, and in the wisdom cell one evening, he was asked if he knew by heart any of the poems of the Columban bards. So he chanted one by the fire in the midst, which spoke of the whole world in a ray of sun.

Triune of Grace,

by holy prayer

of Columb kind,

join me to Thee,

one spirit with Thee.


By Columb's prayers

on angel's mound,

humbly beseeching:

enlarge my heart

as Thou didst him.

Enlarge my heart

to behold as one

the whole world

in a ray of sun,

as Thou didst him.


By holy tears

of a dove of cells,

enlarge my heart:

the whole world

in a ray of sun.


Enlarge my heart

to pray for all,

beholding all

the whole world

in a ray of sun.

Taliesin thanked their guest, and offered a poem of his own in reply, as was the custom. It was composed when he had been in the Isles of the Hebrides some years before.

Isle and sea aflame in Thee,

rock and sand give glory;

wind and surf arise in Thee,

tide and strand cry glory.


Ridge and cliff withstand through Thee,

earth and hearth say glory;

smoke and stone unite in Thee,

peat and flame sing glory.


Turf and thatch enfold through Thee,

stave and door say glory;

butt and ben are lit through Thee,

byre and bed sigh glory.

Cross and cell aflame in Thee,

church and bell give glory;

Brendan, Cormac, Comgall, Kenneth,

with Columcille, cry glory.


Angel wings hov'ring round Thee,

the saints abide in glory;

praising, thanking, circling round Thee,

earth and heaven give glory.


Virgno, delighting to find Taliesin remembered the Isles of the Hebrides in the north, embraced him with great joy. He was fond of bardic poetry, and had heard that Merlin knew something of the Holy Grail. There was a line in one of Columba's poems, *Noli Pater*, which reminded Virgno of the Grail:

'The flame of God's love indwells my heart,

Like a jewel set in gold, placed in a silver grail.'


Virgno said he thought Columba was referring to the Secret of the Grail. Dindrane asked him if Columba knew who serves the Grail and whom the Grail serves. Virgno, pausing for a moment, answered her that it is the pure heart that serves the Grail, and the Grail serves the flame of love indwelling the pure heart, which is the gem set in gold in Columba's poem.

Dindrane nodded, gently smiling. She was glad that Virgno had come among them, and was sharing the wisdom of Columba. She rejoiced that Columba's wisdom was in profound accord with the Pendragon wisdom of Merlin, on the dragon heights of Manstone Mynd.

# 12

# WULFSTAN'S QUEST

A wattle bangor, consisting of a bank and palisade, enclosed Goatshaw Ring on Manstone Mynd. It provided a sacred vallum surrounding the round cells on the hill, and gave to their enclosure a protection that was not of this world. Wattle fences were of no military significance, but marked the sacred boundary that kept dark powers at bay.

Deiniol of Bangor Fawr, on the Menai Straits, had recently built another Bangor at Is Coed, near Wrexham, on the Dee. Both Bangors were fenced wattle enclosures that defined the sacred sanctuary, like forest temples of old. Deiniol's monasteries were centres of learning and prayer, a powerful challenge to warring nether powers. So was Cadfan's monastic centre at Tywyn, founded after he returned from Brittany. Samson had emigrated to Brittany with the blessing of Bishop Dubricius of Archenfeld. Now Cadfan was emigrating from New Britain over Sea, returning to spread Breton wisdom among Britons in Old Britain.

Cadfan's disciples went out from Tywyn to transmit the wisdom of the healing Name, to mend Old Britain's broken, ruined lands. From Gower in the south to Anglesey in the north, the wisdom of the Holy Well in Tywyn reached hearts ravaged by war, including Irish settlers on the western shores.

Cadfan himself went every Lent to Ynys Enlli, called Bardsey Isle by Norse settlers, a sanctuary where Dubricius had recently been buried, and Deiniol and many others would be buried in years to come.

Hywyn of Tywyn went to the Llyn, and built at Aberdaron a monastery there. Lleudadd followed him, and succeeded Cadfan as abbot. Cadfan was buried at Tywyn, as was Cyngen the Renowned, ruler in Pengwern, but their relics were moved to Bardsey, known as isle of twenty thousand saints, sanctuary of hallowing hallows.

It was Lleudadd who met Wulfstan at Pennant, and brought news of an anchorite virgin, Melangell, to Merlin. Melangell, called Monacella by the monks, had escaped from forced royal marriage in Ireland, and fled to Britain, seeking refuge in the Berwyn hills. She held sacred enclosure at Pennant, under the protection of Brochwel, Lord of Powys and Pengwern. A strong community of hermit sisters gathered round Melangell, and Lleudadd was eager to meet them. His visit coincided with that of Wulfstan, abbot of Minster Ley, and it was Wulfstan who related to Lleudadd an account of his neighbours, Merlin and Taliesin.

It was from Lleudadd that Wulfstan learned of Cadfan and the prophets of Tywyn, and of the island sanctuary at Ynys Enlli. Wulfstan, although a Saxon from Mercia, had the utmost respect for Lleudadd, and decided he must meet Cadfan and experience the Holy Well at Tywyn for himself.

So when Lleudadd bade farewell to Melangell, Wulfstan accompanied him to Tywyn, and drank deep from the Holy Well near the Bird Rock estuary, where Taliesin had lived in his youth. Taliesin had been trained in the sanctuary of the bards, imbibing the wisdom of Cadair Idris, the sacred tradition of Druid seers. He had then been young Brochwel's bard for a time, before going north to work for Caledonian kings.

Wulfstan, although a neighbour of Taliesin and Merlin, had not appreciated what Taliesin was doing. It was Cadfan who explained to him that Merlin was a prophet, mage and seer, and that Taliesin was a bard, whose work was the renewal of wisdom and retelling of the myths. Cadfan told Wulfstan that prophecy was crucial to the healing of the land. He said that Deiniol was transmitting healing peace at Bangor in the north. He told Wulfstan of the isle of wisdom in the west, Ynys Enlli, where hallowed hearts quickly turn and see. He explained that the isle was a place of deep seeing, where the glory of the age to come may yet still be seen.

Wulfstan was delighted, and when he returned to his monastery at Minster Ley, it was not long before he made his way round the northern tors to the desert of Manstone Mynd. He met Maeldin, who took him to the wisdom cell, where Merlin and Taliesin were seated in silence round a blazing fire. He related how he had met Lleudadd at Pennant, and seen light in the hearts of the sisters of Melangell, in the enclosure of hermit cells beside Tanat, the sacred stream. He told Taliesin that he had been to the land of his youth, to the foot of the Cadair, Chair of Idris. He spoke of Cadfan's holy well in Tywyn, and the waters of wisdom flowing there, renewing hearts in the midst. He spoke of Deiniol's Bangor, where a healing peace was nourishing the land and curing dolorous wounds.

Taliesin listened, recalling his years at the foot of the Great Chair, where Idris presided over surging tides. The estuary skirted Bird Rock cliff, where cormorants nested and seabirds cried. For him, those lands were sacred to wisdom, redolent with the energies of transmission, powerful with healing that hallowed the land.

Taliesin had accompanied Arthur there when they had journeyed to the netherworld, Annwn, to redeem the cauldron of inspiration, which shares with the Holy Grail the function of hallowed hollow, receptacle of wisdom. Their quest went in search of receptivity to wisdom, capacity for wisdom to indwell them as her dwelling place. For him, the netherworld was sacred, translucent with wisdom, transfiguring ruined hearts. It was a sanctuary where glory is discerned, and where wisdom sustains vision in awakened hearts.

Merlin turned to Wulfstan and told him it was good that he had met Melangell, and that he had travelled with Lleudadd to Tywyn. He knew Cadfan, and Deiniol too. Wulfstan had sought out Merlin to understand better why the work of wisdom was so crucial. Merlin said he wondered if it had occurred to Wulfstan that, as a Saxon of Mercia, perhaps he might begin to undertake this quest of peace, the Matter of Britain, among his own folk, the English of Mercia.

Wulfstan thought for a while and then agreed, but mused with Merlin that if the Matter of Britain were to be communicated to the English, it would at first be perceived as foreign. No Saxon called himself Saxon, because Saxon, Sasanach, meant foreigner in the British tongue. Saxons called themselves Englisc or English, not foreigner. No Briton called himself Welsh, which was the English word for foreigner, but called himself British, or Cumbrian. The Irish called themselves Scots and the Picts called their land Alba, and themselves Cruithni.

If Wulfstan was to transmit the Matter of Britain to his English compatriots, he would need to handle these differences between Britons and English, Picts and Irish. If the legacy of Arthur's British Commonwealth was to become the inheritance of the English, and perhaps also of the Picts and Irish, then Wulfstan was painfully aware he needed not only wisdom, but patience, skill and learning too.

Merlin sensed the importance of this meeting with Wulfstan, but felt utterly at a loss to know how vision of the Throne of Peace, which is ineffable, could ever find expression in such a complex and conflicted world. Yet he knew, somehow, that the peace of the Grail and the Nine Rings was destined to break through. Perhaps it was for others to find a way. Could it be that Nimue, bearer of a ring of light, would discover cures for frozen souls, or Taliesin songs to melt hardened hearts? He did not know.

Britain was heir to far more than old myths and fairy tales. It was heir not only to legends of a once and future king, but to wisdom's vision of light and glory, and the blessing of peace. Archbishop Augustine's mission in Canterbury sought the co-operation of Welsh bishops without success. Britons found the Roman initiative offensive, for what Rome thought it was bringing was already here. Britain looked to Byzantium, seeing the impositions of Rome as perverse.

Merlin could not know that in just a few decades, Cuthbert, Bishop of Lindisfarne, would unite Irish Scots and English Angles in Northumbria, and Archbishop Theodore of Tarsus would unite the English and the British in a peace of the Rood. Peace from the Great Throne was renewing the land, and Merlin laid the foundation of the Matter of Britain by uncovering hallowing Pendragon rings, in the mines of Manstone Mynd.

## 13

# THRONE OF ICE AND STONE

Snow was falling, and the serrated line of the dragon's spine looked like a wall of glacial citadels, amidst pinnacles of shimmering ice. Ganieda was with Wulfstan on the frozen hill, and went round by way of the Needle's Eye to ascend the Throne. Nimue was already there, deep in prayer, aware that as above, so below: the ice above was fire below. Wulfstan watched as Ganieda began to prophesy, for she wore Merlin's mantle at this hour, when glory descended to wed ascending light.

The Throne ascended as the Man in the Stone shone like crystal and glistened with precious gems. Ganieda ascended with the Throne, for its power held her safe, and Wulfstan too, grounded in Nimue's prayer. Descending now, far below, the Throne went down into the mines beneath, where passage caves drove deep into other times and other worlds.

Wulfstan watched as he, too, went down, and Ganieda descended to where the dead were watching. Countless souls were waiting there to rise, battle-worn souls that in war had died together: Briton, Saxon, Angle, Pict. King Rhydderch came towards her as Ganieda turned, half hidden, to face him. Nothing was said. Nothing could be said, for old pain was beyond time or place, so near to joy that glory reigned. The deceased king gazed at his queen and disappeared.

The Throne was glory now, even at these depths, as Mordred emerged from the shadows and Nimue stirred. Was he with the Saxon hordes he joined, or was he among Britons, as Arthur's son, but heir now to another kingdom, not usurped? Insurrection was nowhere now, for the passions of war were enfolding into peace. Wulfstan watched as Horsa rose, with Hengest at his side, and countless Saxon dead. Mordred rose as Arthur rose, reconciled among the stars.

Ynys Enlli opened as Dubricius rose from Bardsey Isle, shepherding Briton and Saxon as one vast shimmering throng. Here, old wars were over, and dissension was issuing into peace. Saint David gathered Britons and Gaels, and Ninian the Briton guided Caledonians and Picts, for the Throne had power to free them now. As the Throne rose, they rose, and broken souls rose with them. All had their place here, forgotten souls whom nobody remembered, and heroes well remembered in the solemn laments of bards. None were excluded, unless they themselves hung back, feeling safe in the shadows, unready to rise.

Mordred was ready, and came with them. Constantine brought Ambrosius and Uther, Lancelot and Gawain, Tristan and Isolde, the unloved and the dearly loved, all were included here in the timeless presence of the Throne. All were embraced by prophecy as Ganieda soared, caught up in the glory of the Man enthroned, one with the Cherubic energies of the Chariot Throne.

Time was no more since all time, future as well as past, was present as remembered presence. Ganieda saw Merlin long ago shape shift as Gandalf, amazed that so many orcs were here, but here as elves. Merlin took form again as Dumbledore greeted Riddle and Potter, both present here in one momentary flash, for Voldemort was no longer in flight from death, now that death was in flight from him.

Tom and Harry, Frodo and Sam, all were here as Merlin was both himself and others, watching over Aragorn's, or was it Arthur's, reign? Ganieda held them all in her heart as they were handed back to the Man. For they were all restored with the Man in the Stone, known now as they were known, in wisdom's dance of the Throne.

Ganieda was prophet now, heir to Merlin and one with prophets still to come. She had come here broken, but wisdom was whole, mothering the hosts in the heart of the Man. Wulfstan watched as she rose with the Throne and went back down, again and again. There was no end to the ascent and descent of the Chariot Throne. There was no end to the love she knew now as her own. There was no end to her mothering of friend and foe, now that peace poured forth from the roots of the Throne.

Wulfstan watched as he beheld her as the Man, as the Stone that danced, the King on the Throne. As he watched, he too became the Man, and danced his dance, for he was the dance when the dance danced him. Wulfstan became the prophet of Saxons by being one with the Man, the Man who turned stone hearts from stone to starry light from his Throne. The Matter of Britain was the matter of peace, and peace mattered to Saxons too.

Nimue held all this in her heart, and pondered it as she returned to her cell. Her heart had been a throne that sustained the Throne intact, through the Man in the Stone. She had stood under the dance and so was in person the dance of the Throne, the dance of love and peace on the frozen tors of Manstone Mynd.

# 14

# GRAIL AND NAME

The Matter of Britain had wedded the Matter of Byzantium when, on Taliesin's return over a year before, the Secret of the Grail unveiled itself to wisdom, unveiling the mystery of the Name. Nimue took both mysteries of Grail and Name and pondered them deep in her heart. That is why she had been able to ground the prophecy of Ganieda on Manstone Mynd. That is how she was ripe to birth Wulfstan's prophecy to the Saxons, as well as Merlin to the Britons, on the Throne. She was an instrument of peace in a land of war.

In regions where endless battles were fought, the land was wracked by the ruin of war. Saxon and Welsh lay buried together, foreigners in each other's tongues, just as in life they were impenitent foes. Saxon and Welsh, enemies in the field, were in death welcomed home beneath the earth. Bones in the earth beneath the feet, wraiths in the waters of the marsh, spirits in fires that consume the dead, and ghosts in the air of all who died too soon, all were torn too suddenly from life's bonds and links of love.

Nimue's heart bore this, all of it, heir to Merlin's elemental work of making peace. The earth of bones, the watery wraiths, the fire of screaming spirits in the anguished air, cried out from the stones for healing. Nimue took Morgana's spells and dissolved them. All bitterness dispelled. Her ring was restored in the waters of the Nine. Morgana's pain unravelled, as Nimue rewove old powers in Avalon. She was inspiration for Taliesin's work of retelling legends so myths could heal. She was empowering mythmaking powers to lead tortured ghosts out of deepest hell, into blessed homes of peace.

Nimue's elven heart had not forgotten that orcs were once elves, and that wraiths were once men, kings of great kingdoms of the sons of men. Her wisdom was not magic that despised muggles, nor was Merlin's wisdom bound by the limits that confined Gandalf, or the exclusions that defined Dumbledore. If she were to inspire Taliesin to rework the myth, it would need to be a peace that delved deeper still.

It would need to be blessing from the Throne, a dance of the Man in the Stone, but it must deal with fissured powers and anguished ghosts, or else Merlin's wisdom would fall short. Impossible for Nimue, such work was light for wisdom. Nimue never claimed to be wise, but to love wisdom.

Nimue knew the wisdom of the Throne and the blessing of peace that reached out from Briton to Saxon. She went to the Throne to uncover mythmaking powers. She took Dindrane with her, by way of the Needle's Eye. She knew Dindrane was whole of heart, and strong in her determination to see the task through to the end, the matter of twin questions: 'Who serves the Grail?' and 'Whom does the Grail serve?' The Grail was empty so that the

Name could fill it, fulfilling twinned quests in graced completeness.

The enemy was not Mordred, or Sauron's orcs, but warring fissured powers that interfered, yet were not real. Nimue knew that orcs were originally elves, so elves were the key to the cure of the rift, the unhealed chasm between wraiths and kings, orcs and men. She could not despise muggles if wisdom was to leaven the whole lump and transfigure what Dumbledore had been unable to transform. The mantle of Merlin had passed to Nimue when, alone on the Throne, she sustained the wisdom that gave Ganieda prophecy and Wulfstan power to wed English foes with Britain, right down to the very depths of hell.

English regions would wed Britain if the axial light in rings of fire and water, earth and air, were permitted to heal the hearts of Britons, who hated Saxon hordes. The English would belong to Britain if the English could open their hearts to the axial light of British wisdom and make it their own. Scots and Picts could be Britons if the myth enlarged its heart as well as theirs. The world would be renewed when wisdom was handed on in such a way that the Name revealed the Man in the Stone on the Throne, and danced together with him his wisdom dance.

Nimue went to the Throne by way of the Eye, entering into the cave at the core of the Throne. Her descent balanced her ascent, healing the rift in the myth, making it whole again. She descended to where the still centre was poised like a drop, axial light at once round and one-pointed, like tear drops, or drops of dew on a leaf, or rain drops renewing life, drop by drop.

Nimue did not stop, but ascended by descending to the fires at the core, the fires where all rings are forged, extinguishing all that obscures. She descended to lower caverns where an ancient alchemy was forever turning lead in the mines to gold. She knew that an elf might turn orcs back into elves, and wraiths into men, if only the purifying ring of fire could be endured, so that the gold could shed the lead. For lead is already gold that half remembers it is gold. The elves are elves even when orcs forget from whence they came. Wraiths are kings and muggles wizards who have forgotten the quest for the pearl.

If only she could acquire eagle's wings and fly, or speak like the letter or the voice in the Song of the Pearl, to remind kings they were kings. The Name would send the dragon to sleep so that the prince could grasp the pearl. Then, in the Name of names, Nimue would wake the dragon and ride it home.

If the pearl was the stone that transformed lead to gold, it must be the wisdom stone. It must be the pentacle stone set in Solomon's ring of wisdom and the Name, which turned the dragon from foe to friend. It was the light of its seal that restored orcs to elves, and it was the glory of the Name that turned wraiths back to kings. Nimue knew that sacred alchemy required Solomon's wisdom, which his Ring transmitted whenever wisdom was welcomed home, in age after age.

While Nimue worked with alchemy, Dindrane remained alone on the Throne until the light that served the Grail dissolved her heart into light, and the glory the Grail served burned as one tongue of flame, releasing her to ascend by descending into the depths of hell.

Then she saw Nimue unite with the Man in the Stone, descending into dark shadows, carrying light to dispel darkness wherever they went. Nimue was Merlin as the Man, turning the stone of the Throne into light, this way and that. For Nimue it was alchemy, turning dull lead into radiant gold. To Dindrane it was love, empowering love, so that in glory, love generates love. There was no argument, but a dance, in which wisdom manifests as different gifts, remedies which work together to heal the whole.

Was it Nimue or Merlin? Was it the Man or the Stone, the Lion or the Throne? Was it ascent or descent? Was it elf or orc, king or wraith? Dindrane could not tell, but knew that light was power enough to undo subservience to fissured powers, that glory was Lion enough to reclaim the Throne. The alchemy of Nimue was working, although how it worked, Dindrane could not say. Nimue could see light generate glory as Dindrane danced, although whether it was Man or Throne that was dancing light, she did not know. She saw that it worked, and that was enough for her.

Dindrane understood that somehow Merlin's work with rings of power was also entrusted to Nimue, so that now the peace of the Nine could be restored. She saw her as a Queen of Stars, surrounded by lights of countless suns, each of which was a ring of fire forging rings of light.

Power lay in a kingdom of liberating light, not in a dominion where domination imposes and abuses power. Dindrane watched with Merlin as Nimue revealed treasures long concealed, swords and rings, and crowns of kings. With Merlin, she was discovering renewing wisdom rings in stars that marked each ring with the Name, giving it power to awaken hearts to wisdom. She saw Nimue take old corrupted rings of power and melt them down in rings of fire that consumed their past on Merlin's funeral pyre.

Dindrane was amazed that Nimue was generating gold from gold, no longer needing to turn lead to gold, because in the fires of starlight, all lead was gold, generating gold from gold. She was aware that Nimue was handling rings of fire, which destroyed delusion wherever she went. She saw, far away in the east, on a holy mountain in Tibet, wisdom give to the King of Ling a throne that rested on a golden ring.

Descending the hill, Dindrane returned to her cell, and watched the full moon rise over the Long Mynd. The stars shone out of the lake of remembrance, and blessed the costly work of peace within Pendragon's Throne, on the tors of Manstone Mynd.

# 15

# WATERS OF AVALON

Nimue the Fay, Lady of the Lake, was fond of a saying of Saint David, Dewi Sant, told her by his foster son, Maedoc of Fern, one of the sons of Gildas:

'Keep the vision and remember the little things.'

Nimue kept the vision in three ways, by turning so as to see, by seeing so as to be, by freeing to be what seeing sees. Turning turns to see. Seeing sees to free. Being is free and freeing, for to be free is to be all that seeing sees. She remembered the little things, because kind vision always remembers and never forgets the little things. Kind vision knows nothing is too lowly to be remembered.

Samthea, her trusted friend, who was a disciple of Brigit of Kildare, told Nimue that Brigit kept the vision by always remembering to love the unloved and unknown. Attention to the little things was crucial for Nimue, as it was for all nine ring-bearers of the Lake. Three of them tended Arthur in Avalon, remembering little things whilst sustaining vision.

One of them, Morgana the Fay, had the capacity to be a great healer, but was wounded in her soul by the birth of Arthur, and by her father's death. Bitter hurt twisted her powers, turning them against her half-brother, Arthur. Seduced by ambivalence, she became a source of confusion and cause of division. Through Morgana, warring powers were let loose and peace was destroyed.

For the Nine, the waters of Avalon were pools of healing vision in which everything was remembered. Nothing was too obscure to be remembered there. Nimue was aware that the Grail and Cauldron of the Netherworld were both receptacles of inspiration, empty for completeness and for peace. Avalon was a sacred Netherland that overlaps with this world, embracing little things so that vision remembered them.

As Nimue descended deeply within healing waters beneath the Throne by way of the Eye, and within the secrets of the Lion by way of the Diamond, light was unveiled beneath the rugged spine of the dragon, dark tors of bright quartz on Manstone Mynd.

Light shone forth from the Throne into the earth of tortured bones, the waters of marsh wraiths, the fires of screaming spirits and the air of anguished ghosts. Light from the Throne was offering elemental healing to all suffering souls through wisdom, and Nimue was Merlin's companion in the work, bringing peace and healing to the land.

Nimue was a Princess of Sarras, City of the Holy Three, delving deep in the midst of the mysteries of the Three. She had studied the triple spiral of the Great Temple on the Boyne, flanked by the hallowed mounds of Knowth and Dowth. She was initiated into the mystery of the Three, conjoined with the Triune mysteries of Byzantium. Virgno had told her that seers from the hill of Tara said the Treskelion was an icon of the Three, opening access to all three centres from creation, and enclosing all three centres in themselves, which was glory enclosed in peace, sharing peace.

Nimue was one of the Nine, whose task was to restore wisdom in Britain. Wisdom's Nether Britain was fair and fay, a land of peace, living from light and glory. It was sustained by vision, for as David, King in Jerusalem, said in his Psalm, it is in light that light is seen. Light was living water that renewed the land. Davidic kings were Stewards of the Lake, guardians of wisdom springs.

Solomon, wisest of them all, tended wisdom springs. He it was who built Jerusalem's temple, in the power of his ring, and welcomed wisdom there. Solomon's ring gave him power to understand the language of all created things, and hear the music of the spheres. Schramir, its jewel, bore the Name and the Star, which bound powers and loosed those bound by powers. The ship of Solomon was wisdom, and it was bound for Sarras, haven of peace in the west.

Nimue, Lady of the Lake, was learned in Davidic gnomic lore, science of light and wisdom. Her work kept vision intact, opening the eye of the heart. Wisdom's netherworld lies within our world, keeping both worlds from falling apart. Wisdom is loving remembrance, embracing enemies as friends, in the healing waters of Avalon. Nimue learned from Merlin how wisdom's work was done, but it had always been her destiny, her calling prior to her birth into this world. Merlin discerned it, but he did not cause it. He was wisdom's midwife, and so was she.

Nimue was light from the Lake of Light, waters of light rising as mists of peace, which veil and unveil glory. But glory knows that lake and mists are one. When the lake rises, it is mist, which veils and unveils at once. Glory reveals things as they are. The waters of Avalon mother the poetic making that remakes things into what they were always meant to be. The Lake mothers the wisdom of bards. Nimue rode waves of stars, partaking in the making. The scope of wisdom in nine rings of Avalon was the sphere of beauty in the Netherworld. Heaven meets earth in Nether Britain, image of the summer stars.

Arthur was betrayed, betraying and betrayed, but Merlin's work was never done, undoing fissured powers in netherworlds. Arthur's peace glimpsed true peace, but Britain only truly weds her Saxon enemies in Sarras, where the Grail is found.

The peace of Sarras severs vainglory to wed glory in the glorious Name. The English were written into Britain by the pen of bards, not forced by the sword of warrior kings. Byzantium appeared under the dome of Sophia, but staggering, due to dolorous wounds. Doom was golden for the seer, but fleeting, like a unicorn. The bard returned to the Lake, and Nimue was there, glory weaned off vanity by rings of fire, to keep open the Eye to the Throne.

Nimue was imbibing the wisdom of the Nine in the waters of the Lake. Avalon's power of vision and remembrance unravelled the fatal charms of warring elemental powers. The wisdom waters of the Lake dissolved divisive separation. The flame of ringed fire severed confusion with a two-edged sword. The healing earth crystallized what the waters dissolved, so that mists of hallowed air, restoring confusion to healthy union, purified all impure powers.

Avalon awakened Pendragon wisdom, marked by the precision of vision. The waters of wisdom were able to undo the contortions of fissured powers, because what is above has power to heal what is below. There was no healing on the plane of ruptured powers themselves. Only wholesome energies can heal. Only wholesome peace can make peace beneath the Throne.

On the Throne, Nimue was fulfilling Merlin's functions now, and Merlin was fulfilling the Man Stone's wisdom, one with Enoch and the Son of Man. Nimue rode the dragon, for the dragon was friend not foe. She saw things with the dragon's eye, as Merlin had, whose Pendragon wisdom began where it ended, like coiled dragons whose mouths consumed their tail. She watched as watchers turned and saw the energy rise in endless circles, which cured all dolorous wounds.

The Fisher King rose from his bed, his sickness cured, his wound healed. Everywhere the Grail was revealing its secret, unveiling the light that serves the Grail, unfolding the glory the Grail serves. It was not that Nimue laid claim to anything special, or presumed to answer Grail questions that haunted knights long ago. It was that the questions answered themselves as the Grail found itself, as the Man in the Stone unfroze himself. Wisdom found her dwelling place in the Lake where she was really at home. The mist veiled her mysteries from being profaned.

Nimue was Avalon in person, from whom healing remembrance flowed. She was one with Merlin as he worked his wisdom, forging golden rings of peace, renewing the ruined land. She was one with Taliesin and the inspiration of bards, offering light to the eyes of their hearts so they could sing. On her own, she was broken and small, but through wisdom she was wholeness renewing the ruined, broken land. She did not belong to herself, but to all, in all, for all. She was a messenger of Sarras, City of the Grail, Sarras in person, weaving golden peace by transmitting the twinned wisdom of the Holy Three.

Nimue saw Avalon's waters generate rings of light, turning orcs to elves and wraiths to kings, whose kingdoms had been in ruin whilst their dark lords were in flight from death. Death fled them as Nimue watched, as watchers in every generation were restored, remade, renewed.

As wisdom made all things new in Avalon, Enoch and the watchers were listening all over the world. The wisdom of Mar Thoma's twin was here on the Mynd as the Man, the Son of Man, the Man in the Stone. Solomon's Ring was overpowering divisive powers, building temples in awakened hearts in Avalon. Here, David's Star was wedding stars and stones in Merlin's heart.

Avalon's Lake of remembrance was restoring the land, in the caves beneath Manstone Mynd.

# 16

# PEACE WEAVERS

Nimue the peace weaver now danced a wisdom dance, the dance of peace of the Man in the Stone. The Throne raised hells to heavens in her heart, to hallow the Name and heal the land. She was a weaver of peace in red-gold rings, bright netherworlds brought nigh in hallowed things. In her, wisdom was at home, so that what wisdom was, she was, in loving ways. Wisdom was so near that she was nearer than near to every heart, before they turned, so that when they turned, she was there to welcome them to vision.

Dindrane sensed that Nimue had changed. She wore the same appearance but the energy she bore was different. A Throne of peace was alight right here in her heart. Dindrane saw in Nimue a light that shone in her, a glory leaping from heart to heart. Love flowed forth to gather to itself all those who welcome love, so they might heal. Avalon's waters beneath the Throne were rivers of light that Dindrane experienced as love.

The Grail showed Dindrane that her own heart too was the Manstone Throne, and the Eye that turns and sees. Her twinned questions were resolved, for the light that serves the Grail and the glory the Grail serves were dancing as one ring of light. Here in her midst, one glory was unveiled in many kings and many rings.

Dindrane and Nimue were not alone. Ganieda also was prophet, mage and seer, able to be the word she spoke, so as to walk the talk of wisdom. Maeldin was a living spring, whose waters never ceased to flow.

The companions gathered in the wisdom cell, where Taliesin conversed with Merlin whilst their hearts were plunged into silence, still at centre in the midst. Was this a gathering of men or women, elders or angels? Were these ring-wrights or Grail seers, ring-bearers or unsuspecting kings?

Merlin had invited Wulfstan to join them, to discover how the Matter of Britain now fared among the English, and whether the British were willing to enlarge their hearts to embrace the Saxon hordes. Wulfstan had been travelling in Old Britain, and in new Saxon lands. He had been to New Britain over Sea, and found that Bretons, like Britons, were beginning to heal, opening to light beyond ruin, welcoming inklings of glory when stars wed stones.

The problem was that minds were out of accord with hearts, divided by fear. Hearts might see for a moment but minds were cut off. When it came to the test, divided minds won out and obscured the heart. He found that whilst the Columban peace wedded Pict and Scot in the north for a while, it did not last. In the south, British and English were making treaties that barely held them back from war.

Merlin responded that it seemed to him that to win the Battle for Britain, wisdom must win minds as well as hearts, awakening Briton and Saxon, Jute and Pict. It required the British to leap over old fears into an illumined heart, for the heart could not enlarge if the mind was closed. Hardened hearts were blind and deaf to what the senses cannot see. How was peace to weave a way into minds in accord with hearts? How was war to turn from foes without to the old pain within that betrays them all, ruptured powers whose deceit holds hearts in thrall.

Taliesin remarked that the myth was not at fault, only the way the tales were told. If the myth was serving blind hearts, the myth became blind. If wisdom opened the eyes of the blind, hearts would turn and see. How could the myth be retold, so that it awakened hearts and opened the eyes of the blind? If the Grail served glory, it was only because light served the Grail. How was wisdom to be transmitted, not only in this, but in any age?

'By renewal of prophecy,' said Ganieda.

'Prophecy and prayer,' said Dindrane. 'Without prayer, prophecy falls on stony ground and cannot take root.'

'What was it that was healing in the bluestone circle?' asked Nimue. Without waiting for an answer, she continued: 'It was not the stone sarsens of the Henge that healed, but the bluestone circle within the Henge. It was the bluestones that gathered the wounded and the sick. That is why bluestones were chipped away, year upon year, from age to age, by those who came for healing. The bluestone heals because it is the grey-green earth shot through with summer stars. The heavens stoop to kiss the earth and the earth returns the kiss for all eternity. It is written in the stones. The voice of the stones is prophecy, and the silent kiss of stars is prayer.'

Merlin knew the union of stars and stones was the union of heaven and earth, of all invisible as well as visible worlds. It lay at the heart of the wisdom of the Healing Henge, of elders in the Elder Days of barrows and the hunt.

'It was the secret of the kiss of stars and stones,' he said, 'as well as the gaze and the embrace.'

'That is the wisdom of Mary Magdala,' said Dindrane.

'Melangell and the sisters at Pennant know of this, as you, Wulfstan, are aware. It is the kiss of stars and stones that nestles in the heart of the Son of Man. Magdala's Mary knew.'

'The language of the bards is the healing power of metaphor,' said Taliesin. 'The two are one, yet the one remains two, when the gaze and the kiss embrace. Luminous stones are mirroring summer stars. The bluestone wisdom of the Healing Henge was at the heart of the older wisdom of elders, barrows and the tombs. It returns as the gaze, the kiss and the embrace, Solomon's Temple mysteries enshrined in his star-sealed Ring from Old Jerusalem, transmitted by Byzantium. It returns as a Song of Songs through the Name.'

'Wisdom is recognized by her own,' said Merlin. 'She is loved and known by those who welcome her. She withdraws when she is not received, but returns when she finds a dwelling place. She is wedded to those who are embraced by her gaze, and who return her kiss.' Merlin paused, and then Taliesin spoke:

'There is no end to the madness of war and ruin, until wisdom's gaze and kiss are embraced. Philip, in his Gospel, spoke of this, and Mary Magdala too, but eyes were blind and hearts were deaf. Their Gospels were forgotten, and all that was left in these isles until now was rumour of the Grail.'

Wulfstan listened as peace weavers were making peace, and realized in his heart that peace can only come from peace, not war. He saw that if peace was reactive, it remained a weapon of war. He knew it was in peace that Byzantium prayed for peace, as wisdom's Liturgy taught her long ago. Her litanies were wisdom's peace praying for peace, both as prophecy and prayer.

Merlin was weaving peace by hallowing the Name on Solomon's Ring, which welcomed home in peace the wisdom of Byzantium. Saxon ring-bearer among Britons, Wulfstan was inspiring renewing rings of peace amidst ravaged rings of war. Merlin's peace wove dragon claws into Pendragon rings, on the tors of Manstone Mynd.

# 17

# MERCIAN ADVANCE

Between the battles of Badon and Camlann, Arthur's three decades of wise sovereignty had brought peace to Pengwern. Mercians were advancing on Caer Guricon, white city of the wildwood wolds, but they were open to treaty with Cornovian Britons.

The ruler of Pengwern in Arthur's reign had been Cyngen the Renowned. It was Brochwel, Cyngen's son, who signed a treaty with Mercia and who presided at this time over the peace of Pengwern. It was Brochwel who gave Pennant to Melangell, and who offered Merlin protection on Manstone Mynd, and gave lands in the forests for the monastery at Minster Ley.

The Cornovians had permitted peaceful Mercian settlement on their eastern borders for decades, and Wulftsan had travelled among them and found them open to Merlin's peace. The Mercians for their part showed no sign of attacking their Cornovian neighbours, and when British kings went to war with one another in the west, they did not interfere.

Wulfstan concurred with Gildas that British kings lost the Battle of Britain in the north because war between Britons wreaked havoc and ruin in Cumbria and Caledonia. The Northumbrian English now ruled Britons in the northeast, and

Mercians were a powerful dynasty in the Middle Lands, ruling many British, whom they called Welsh.

The Cornovians of Pengwern were British, but many of them were happy to live in the east, as Welsh under Mercian rule, just as, in the west, Mercian Saxons like Wulfstan were living under British rule. There was Britain, and there were English regions, but not yet England, and it was Merlin's vision and Wulfstan's quest to extend Arthur's peace to English regions so that the Matter of Britain might embrace the English too.

In Pengwern, all folk were foreigners to someone, and 'them' and 'us' meant both more and less than elsewhere. Saxons were English among Britons, and Welsh were Britons under English rule. Here on the borders, where many fault lines met, the Pengwern Marches were defined by war, but also by a peace transmuting war, which came to be known as Merlin's peace.

Saxon and Welsh lived side by side in Pengwern, watching English and British forces wage war elsewhere. Saxon and Welsh were often bilingual here, speaking both English and British, called Welsh by the English. Dynasties came and went, but the folk that came to the Wrekin Moot were English and British, who called each other Saxon and Welsh.

The northern border of Greater Mercia was the river Trent, with Northumbrian Angles to the north, East Angles and South Saxon folk to the east, and West Saxons to the south. Mercia contained many small kingdoms, but gradually the ancient dynasty of Icel's crown extended the reign of Iceling kings. Tributary princes like Brochwel continued to rule their lands, but under the sovereign reign of Iceling kings. The Icelingas of Mercia were strong and their power lay in the ruling rings of Iceling English kings.

The Mercian kings called themselves Anglian kings in Britain, not kings of England, and Merlin called Arthur's sovereignty and peace the Matter of Britain, not of England. Manstone was English and Mynd was British, but Manstone Mynd was both, and the Man in the Stone was neither.

All agreed Pengwern was a haven of peace when Brochwel reigned in Caer Guricon. Some said Pengwern meant the headwaters of the Gwern, or Severn, the upper reaches of the great river near the Cornovian capital Caer Guricon. Some thought Pengwern meant hill above the Wern, referring to the Wrekin, hill moot where folk of the Wroken met.

When Caer Guricon was no longer defensible, being too far east, Brochwel moved the Pengwern court northwest for a time to Salopia. Here, the waters of the Gwern strengthened his defences on all sides except northeast, where the earthworks were. If, originally, the Pen of the Gwern meant the headwaters of the Gwern, the Pen could now mean the fortified hill protected by a wide bend in the Gwern. Some called the river Wern the Gwern, whilst in the west it was called Havren, and in the east, the Severn. For Merlin it bore the waters of Avalon to the southern seas.

The loss of Caer Guricon ruined Viroconium, but not the legacy of Merlin's Arthurian peace. Cyngen's bounty, inherited by Brochwel, gave Melangell sanctuary, and Pennant became a centre of pilgrimage imparting peace. Cyngen's renowned Queen, Tudlwysti, was still revered in Powys and Pengwern, and her grandson, Tysilio, was remembered in Meifod, Anglesey and Brittany. Both were saints of Powys and Pengwern. Cornovian Britons revered their legacy, which preserved Pendragon peace.

Merlin's peace forged red-gold rings and crowns of kings, less easily remembered than haloes, in centuries that lost touch with wisdom. Nonetheless, his rings of fire called forth poetic diction in later times. Merlin's witness at the crack of doom discerned the difference between the wisdom of the mage and counterfeits, conjured by power-obsessed sorcery. Self-interested magicians saw Merlin as the dupe of kings, because wisdom was invisible to them.

Merlin was prophet, mage, and seer, who served wisdom and whom wisdom served, not slave of a dark lord's lust for power, or pinion of an oblivious ring. Merlin clearly saw that ring quests were no longer in search of rings of power, as in the Age of Bronze or Iron. He was baffling to sorcerers, as his wisdom was to kings. Merlin knew who served the Ring, and whom the Ring served. Throne vision, like a ring of fire, turned rings of power into radiant rings of peace, unveiling stars in treasure stones, on the slopes of Manstone Mynd.

# 18

# BLACK DRAGON TORS

Merlin remembered the dragon wars beneath the tors of Dinas Emrys, and they reminded him of Pendragon wars beneath the tors of Manstone Mynd. The black dragon at the heart of the Throne was thinly veiled to him, for he knew it on the inside as two, red and white, fierce and bright, locked in terrible struggle for the Sceptre and the Crown.

But as he watched, by way of Eye and Throne, he suddenly saw that what young Merlin had seen as war was not war at all, but an embrace of love. The red dragon was lovingly riding the white, locked in ravaging embrace. They wrestled in ecstasy as both red and white rose to orgasmic climax and were still. A heart of light lay within the embracing dragons, red and white. It spoke of love, not war.

Both red and white were dragons of the Throne, and the Lake beneath was where they loved and sighed. The tors of the black dragon's spine were cherubic swords guarding an inner paradise from profane wars. None could enter there except dragon seers, knowing the glory of the dragon's heart. Outside, black tors loomed, but from within, there shone the glory of the Throne. Solomon's Ring guarded the Holy of Holies as a Bridal Chamber long ago. Pendragon rings watched over a conjugal embrace of dragons red and white, which concealed yet revealed a Cherubic Throne.

Merlin was aghast. How had he missed this all these years? Was it just a young man's foible to see love's wrestle as war? Would everything not have been quite different if he had seen not war but love? If this was the Holy of Holies, beneath the Throne, what was the point of deceiving Igraine to fulfil Uther's desire? Royal bloodlines were beside the point if Pendragon war was really a Pendragon embrace. All could have been different if he had seen not war but love's embrace, Solomon's Bridal Chamber veiled in the Holy of Holies.

Merlin gazed in shock, as the dragons lay entwined, red and white, coiled and bright, at peace beneath the throne. Pendragon union in the depths of the Lake now stared him in the face. The Throne was safe, the foundation sure, but charged with dragon energy, entwined and intertwining. Arthur's reign was no longer locked into fault-line wars or set in frozen stone.

Blazing quartz hid beneath black tors, white light shone at the heart of blood red wars. Merlin had seen dark as dark and not as light. He had seen war as war and not as love, and so made war serve love and love serve war. That was the tragedy of Camelot, and its loves had ended in war.

Now he saw tors veiling dragons red and white, conjoined in a love embrace of light, so what he had seen as war was really love, making all the difference in the world. Instead of love serving war, and war serving love, love not war was wisdom's way, now that wisdom's war was love. The same phenomena, the same myth, but a sudden shift, a timeless lift, rose soaring aloft into a vast expanse, a luminous cloud, a ring of fire, a transfigured myth, a transformed world.

Merlin was dumbstruck as awe, laughing, saw blazing red carnelian and freezing white quartz wedded at the heart of serrated tors. This was the wisdom of the Great Peace. This was Pendragon peace that was not at war with anything, not even war.

Merlin, wondering, mused in his heart as the vision was kneaded in. He knew this was the Pendragon key to the mysteries of the Great Peace. He saw Pax Romana, besieged by war, engender war from war. He saw Pax Britannica, no longer confined by war, generate love from love, by fire, engendering love.

As he watched, he saw Melangell meet with the Man on the Throne and realized, with surprise, that she was already alive to mysteries of peace. The Tanat springs and cataracts were wisdom springs of peace. Merlin saw war constraining Melangell's uncle, Rydderch Hael, Ganieda's warrior husband, and the lords of Cumbria. He saw war confining Melangell's royal family from Tudwal Tudclud. An inheritance of war determined both royal houses, for all her forebears were Irish kings, warrior lords of war.

But Melangell's vision was peace. Her anchorhold at Pennant was a protected haven of peace. She held Cwm Pennant from Brochwel, Tysilio's father, with rights of asylum, refuge and defence. Tame hares flocked to her. Melangell's lambs sought peace, sisters who sought sanctuary with her, safe from rape and ruin. Her cell nestled in a sacred grove of seven yews. Here, fugitives claimed sanctuary and found peace. Merlin saw that Melangell was already heir to wedded dragons and a throne of peace.

He saw Gwyddfarch in his desert above Meifod, a hilltop hermit with a heart of peace. He realized he, too, was living a union of dragons beneath the Throne. His cell on Anchorite's Hill was a bed of rock that opened deep into the Lake beneath, where dragon's war was dragon's peace. Merlin saw Meifod, the royal sepulchre of Powys and Pengwern, and Beuno was with Tysilio there, inspired like him by peace. The vast six-acre vallum of the Powys kings was spread below, and Gwyddfarch's Church welcomed Tysilio and his cousin, Asaph, by law of sanctuary. Tysilio, Brochwel's heir, met here with Deiniol, his friend, choosing peace instead of war.

Merlin saw the throne of Cyngen was Brochwel's now, so when Tysilio, his heir, fled to Gwyddfarch, the king was wrath, for he had trained him in war to preserve the peace. So Tysilio fled to the Menai Straits, founding Llandyssilio, an isle of peace. Gwyddfarch's peace stood firm, and eventually Tysilio returned to be abbot in his stead, for the elder was now old.

Iago, Tysilio's brother, succeeded Brochwel after his father's bloody defeat at Chester. Iago died, leaving his widow, Haiarnwedd, who tried to force Tysilio to her throne and bed. With Gwiddfarch dead, and his peace dead with him, Tysilio, unprotected, was forced to flee again, this time to Brittany. Haiarnwedd's plight drove him overseas. As Suliau, Tysilio was remembered in Brittany, a prince of peace indeed. He never returned, but sent his staff with the Gospels, as his remembrance. He bore witness to a union of dragons in Brittany and a throne of peace in Britain.

Merlin saw Erfyl, daughter of Padarn, friend of David and Teilo, slain beside an ancient yew. She was only thirteen years old. Her memorial stone by the yew, and her church, Llanerfyl, remembered her. It was said it was her staff that still lived on in the form of that aged yew. Here, her tree showed where death was life, and war peace. A well nearby was a healing spring with waters from a lake of wedded dragons, beneath a throne of peace.

Merlin saw countless saints and sanctuaries springing from the Throne, witnesses to renewing peace. Wedded dragons lay hid beneath the armoured spine of tors. He saw Cadfan in Tywyn inspiring hearts with wisdom at Llangadfan, unveiling souls to glory in Ynys Enlli, isle of saints beyond the Llyn.

He saw Beuno in the north with Teilo and David in the south, bringing peace to east and west. He saw Gildas berating tyrants, unaware that he spoke in the name of Merlin's wedded dragons. His son, Maedoc, was witness with David to a Throne of peace. He saw Cadoc at Llancarfan, welcoming Gildas, thanking him for inspiring saints to make peace instead of ruinous war.

Merlin saw Padarn founding Llanbadarn Fawr, inspiring hearts with peace in the west, before retiring to a hermitage at Nant y Mynach in the north. Merlin saw Dyfrig at peace with his brethren in Hentland, before he became Bishop Dubricius of Archenfeld. He saw Padarn with Teilo and David in Jerusalem, founding British bishoprics, but also imbibing there the wisdom of the Name, like Taliesin in Byzantium. The bishoprics could now prove their independence from Canterbury, but the Name tuned hearts to wisdom rings of peace.

Merlin was amazed. He had saved his skin and impressed King Vortigern, only to make love serve war. He had mistaken love for war, and instituted a golden age of love and war. But Merlin was also witness to wedded dragons making love not war. Peace was everywhere inspiring peace, the Pendragon Pax of Manstone Mynd.

# 19

# TWINS IN GEMINI

Merlin had discovered the twin dragons of the Manstone Throne. The red dragon was key to the flaming Stone, and the white dragon key to the white-gold crowning of the Pendragon Throne. Taliesin saw it in Merlin, Merlin found it in Taliesin. Neither of them grasped it on their own, as their own. It would burn them if they tried.

The resilient wisdom of Merlin was reciprocated by the resonant music of Taliesin. They were as twins who danced the wisdom dance of Yeshuah and Mar Thoma, his twin, to heal the dolorous wound of warring twins, Balin and Balan.

Merlin and Taliesin were twin seers of the sacred house of Gemini, twins who were undoing the ambivalence of twinned oblivion. Ignorant twins spawned incoherence from confusion, but wise twins wove co-inherence out of confusion. Mirroring twins twinned heaven and earth in mysterious ways. King Pelles bled in Carbonek, mirroring the red wound on Jupiter, planet of the kings. Arthur bled in Avalon, mirroring the red wound on the Sun, and the bleeding king in Jerusalem.

Merlin knew he was nicknamed Lailoken of the wildwood in some parts, and Emrys his twin in others. He was known as Prince Myrddin in the region of Carmarthen, and as the child of a dark spirit and a virgin nun. Still others claimed he was of the royal house of Gwynedd and others that he was mad, but not all twins discerned the wisdom of twinned seers who see.

Merlin's first love was love of wisdom, and of wisdom's cures of the ambivalence of ignorance, here on Manstone Mynd. The difference between ambivalence and wisdom concerned him, because Balin killed Balan in ignorance, and struck the fatal blow that dealt the dolorous wound. Arthur slept with his sister Morgause in ignorance, and Mordred was born, who killed Arthur. Ignorance spawned confusion, which brought doom through ambivalence. Merlin was wrestling with the fatal ambivalence of twins and siblings, because it parodied the mysteries of wisdom. The cure was co-inherence that could undo confusion, wisdom that could heal ambivalence.

Taliesin was here to redeem the myth. He had seen legends degenerate to become deadly poison. He had seen symbols wreak havoc when separation tore both myth and land apart. The king's poet held wise paradox together in poems. He sang wisdom songs, lest the paradoxical whole fell apart. Taliesin took care that his song was not diction that separates, seduces and destroys. The king's poet wedded sense and spirit, building the City of the Grail. Taliesin's poetry mirrored the creativity of the Word, when it made the Word flesh and Spirit sense, over and over again. Wisdom song hallowed the land.

Merlin was wrestling with the nightmare of twinned ambivalence in the lower deeps. What mattered was release from mirroring destructive powers that confused and deceived. What he was here to undo was the ignorance that led to ambivalence, which dealt the dolorous wound. He was here to apply the remedies of healthy wisdom to heal the fatal flaw. He was here to transmit Pendragon wisdom, whose seers wove peace, redeeming times and worlds.

Taliesin sometimes saw Manstone Mynd as an isle, surrounded in mist like a vast sea. The tors were at once dark and menacing, yet concealed luminous white quartz within. He saw that the surrounding horizon at once separated and united stars and stones, just as his poems at once separated and united heaven and earth. The mist of Avalon concealed waters from the interference of ambivalence, preserving wisdom at the heart of vision stones.

Merlin's companions on Manstone Mynd were not closed, like a clique of like minds. They were a remnant that kept vision alive, a gathering of shepherds who loved and transmitted wisdom. They were companions of wisdom's co-inherent rings that wedded each in all and all in each. The Grail was a virgin womb for their rebirth to happen in, and the womb of their hearts was a Grail from which wisdom's life-blood would flow forth.

For Taliesin, the war of rings was an Iron Age obsession that would never end until warring rings were wedded to a Rood. Rings could wed only if they were crossed. The Ringed Rood, which was later called a Celtic Cross, united the rings of henges and barrows with the Rood of Roman Britain. The legacy of

Constantine's Britain was a union of ringed stars and cross-inscribed stones, as in old Byzantium.

Taliesin knew he was only one of many bards, all of whose brows were radiant. Most of them would follow him and serve the Ringed Rood. He knew there was nothing special about him. It was absurd, this wisdom, absurd but glorious. It was so everyday and ordinary, yet glorious with a greatness that was ineffable. It stretched his powers as a bard, so when poetic diction fell short, he sang wisdom songs of a Ringed Rood.

Merlin saw the Stone in the Man and the Man in the Stone, in stars as well as stones, here on Manstone Mynd. He knew the twinned wisdom of the Stone was everywhere. Recognition not sensation opened doors to the tors. Brochwel's protection was a prison for Tysilio, so he fled, but for Merlin it was a refuge to which he fled, paradoxical but sure.

Taliesin recognized the grit of broken tors might appear absurd to many. Absurd: the mud, the mist, the drizzle and rotting autumn leaves. But if shattered bone, veiling the Man alight in broken stone, appears absurd, it was glorious too. Here, love that seeks not its own pointed to a hidden alchemy, the wisdom in old stones. The stone grounds wisdom, but wisdom grinds the stones. The diamond stone cut through to the Lion, and the Lion Stone gave strength to Eye and Throne.

It was all here, hidden in the stones, yearning to be loved and known. It was present in the tors, once the Eye gave access to the Throne. Voldemort fled death by investing his soul in rings and things, but here on the Throne, once turning sees, death flees him. Taliesin retold the myth again, forging twinned vision rings to give fresh life to legend, making room in the myth for wisdom, for her indwelling.

The tales of Vortigern's collapsing citadel on Dinas Emrys, and of Merlin's supervision of the construction of the bluestone ring within the Henge, were all common gossip in Merlin's day. Whether Merlin helped Uther to deceive Igraine to father Arthur was of no interest to Taliesin.

Pendragon wisdom was what mattered to Taliesin. Merlin's engendering of Arthur's Britain mattered, the sword in the stone and the Round Table mattered, for they were symbols of Pendragon wisdom, embedded at the heart of the Matter of Britain.

Merlin took no notice of those who said that he was infatuated with Nimue, and that she deceived him into divulging all his spells, which she then used against him. Nimue was no envious witch, but there is no surprise that gossip is twisted when driven by envy and revenge.

The tale that he awoke to prophecy amidst deep trauma, Merlin did not deny. He was here to heal from Mordred's treachery, and from the useless ruin of sibling wars. He was here to cure madness caused by Morgause's poisoned apples, apples that Maeldin ate, that had been meant for him.

Merlin remembered the Round Table of Arthur, now entrusted to seers, the Round Table of Joseph, entrusted to prophets, concealed in Arimathea. He remembered the Round Table of the Upper Room, where apostles received mysteries of graced union, bequeathing symbols of light and glory like the Holy Grail. The Ring was hidden in Merlin's care. The Grail and the Lance were concealed in Carbonek, but the Shroud was safe in Abgar's City of Edessa, in the Cathedral Church of Holy Wisdom.

To Merlin, hallows were sacred in the eyes of Pendragon wisdom, because they were fruit of the same union as dragons beneath the Throne. Hallows were charged with healing power, the renewing power of wisdom twins. Stones beneath the Throne had different powers. Vision Stones were in touch with each other and with rings of power and peace, watched over in delved deeps inaccessible to curious scrutiny.

What mattered to Merlin was Pendragon healing beneath the Throne, and the Matter of Britain, twinned wisdom of the stones. Seeing Stones in Edessa were aware of the Shroud, and of stones in Jerusalem linked to Solomon's Ring. Stones gave Merlin vision in Byzantium and India, at the healing Henge and in Sarras. Pendragon wisdom stones watched over twinned rings of power, keeping Merlin mindful of the wisdom of star-stone seers. Wisdom stones saw through the quartz to twinned wisdom, uniting what divides, in caves of the Throne on Manstone Mynd.

# 20

# GALAHAD'S ASCENT

Dindrane's way of love led her beyond images, whereas the way of the king's poet, Taliesin, embraced images and the imageless vision of wisdom they both shared, here on Manstone Mynd. This difference led them to go their separate ways for a time, she to the cloister at Amesbury, he to Camelot. But the catastrophe of Camlann had brought them together, as had the Grail, and the twin questions: 'Who serves the Grail?' and 'Whom does the Grail serve?'

Dindrane had discovered the light that serves the Grail, through beholding light in Taliesin, and Taliesin had awoken to the glory the Grail serves, by beholding love's glory in Dindrane.

Ascetic ascent met mystic descent in equal balance in Dindrane and Taliesin, wedding love's sacred image and love's imageless vision in a union of hearts. They had parted and met again many times over the years, and were now free of fixation, whether they were together or apart. They were at peace in freedom and surrender. There was no dithering, no hesitation. In them, the light that knows who serves the Grail loved the glory that knows whom the Grail serves.

Galahad, son of Lancelot, was born from confusion, for Lancelot thought Elaine was Guinevere. Brisen's dark enchantment spawned ambivalence. Confusion reigned and division brought deep suffering. Lancelot went out of his mind, and was like a wolf in the wilderness. Young Galahad was brought to Amesbury where he was reared under Dindrane's tender eye. Percival and Bors entrusted the child to her, until he came of age. The sisters of Amesbury loved him, and taught him all they knew.

When, in accordance with prophecy, Galahad left for Camelot, Dindrane retained a mother's concern for him. When he drew the sword from the stone and sat at the Round Table, in the Seat Perilous, she left Amesbury to be near him. She was in Camelot when the Grail appeared and he was chosen to go in quest of it.

Many thought Dindrane died helping Percival, Bors, and Galahad find the Grail, but she recovered and withdrew into the forest. Galahad anointed the wounded Fisher King, descendent of Joseph of Arimathea, with blood from the Lance of Longinus. Galahad, a holy knight, brought healing to Britain's ruined wasteland, and it was then that Merlin hid in Caledonia's wilderness.

Taliesin knew that Galahad's success was Lancelot's loss from the beginning. The fact of Galahad's birth drove Lancelot mad, wild as a wolf. The Grail inspired quests, but fay shadows brought destruction in their wake. Grace was not bound to wound nature, but when ascent is violent, harrowed wounds cry out. Why did Grail quests destroy the ascenders? Mothers and elders cried: 'Why do you wound us so? We seek you, sorrowing. Ascend, by all means, but then descend, embracing all.'

When Dindrane heard Gawain had told Arthur of Lancelot's love for Guinevere, she realized Mordred, Gawain's half-brother, was jealous for revenge. She grieved when civil war then rent Camelot's blessed commonwealth in two. She was powerless when Arthur's quest for the Grail took him abroad and left Mordred regent. She was helpless when, in the vacuum caused by Arthur's absence, Mordred usurped the king. After Camlann, Dindrane fled north to find Taliesin, and joined him in the Caledonian wolds.

Dindrane was painfully aware of the irony of Galahad's ascent, which bred Britain's catastrophic rejection of descent. She knew descent wed to ascent was crucial. Her work on the questions of the Secret of the Grail balanced ascent into light with descent by glory. That was why she insisted there were two Grail questions and not, as some taught, just one.

Taliesin read Pendragon union back into the myth, balancing twinned ascent with descent, transforming incoherence in the lore of bards. Dindrane and Taliesin lived Pendragon union of stars and stones, wed with wisdom's Ring of Oneness. Conjoining dragons at the heart of rings of fire, they knew that ignorant force or fear could not actually usurp the Ring, for it was a Ring of radiant Oneness.

But fear had power, and force might parody oneness by conjuring one counterfeit ring to rule and bind the rest. Delusions could conjure parodies that fed the deceptions of dark sorcerers, but could be dissolved where they were forged.

Merlin's work with dragon heirloom rings was to extract their poison to release their energy in wisdom. The Great Ring of Oneness ensured ruptured powers could not interfere with vision stones or obstruct rings of wisdom. Solomon's Ring bore a star and the Name, veiling what it unveiled through wisdom.

Elders in the Elder Days felt they were under siege from dark lords with rings of power, using counterfeit rings to insinuate fear and secure dominion. In the Age of Iron, they thought wraiths haunted the stones, whilst dragons were obsessed with hoards, which fed their obsession with wars and rings.

But Merlin and Nimue, Taliesin and Dindrane, worked with a different power, securing rings of power with vision stones. The Ring of Oneness purified rings of power with rings of fire, leaving Taliesin free to sing wisdom songs of rings and vision stones. Merlin was witness to warring dragons wed in caves beneath the Throne, communicating light from the depths and peace from the heights of Manstone Mynd.

# 21

# BROCHWEL'S LAMENT

Brochwel's lament for the loss of his son pierced those who knew him to the bone. Brochwel's lament for the loss of his heir was as fierce as if Tysilio had died in battle. His lament was fiercer still because his loss was due to another kind of death, a death to war inspired by peace.

Gwyddfarch's peace inspired Tysilio to flee the court, claiming sanctuary in Meifod, Gwyddfarch's hermitage near Brochwel's hunting retreat. Brochwel was generous to the saints, as his father, Cyngen, and Tudlwysti, his saintly Queen, had been. He loved the Church and gladly supported men of prayer.

Brochwel gave lands at Meifod to Gwyddfarch to be his hermitage. He had given Pennant to Melangell, and Minster Ley to Teilo and Wulfstan. But this was different. This was his son and heir, renouncing his inheritance, now as good as dead to him. Brochwel felt wounded and his lament was fierce. Taliesin, who knew him, was concerned for his friend.

Taliesin had been Brochwel's bard many years before, and understood the world of warrior kings. It was one thing to be generous to hermit saints, but quite another to lose a son and heir to them. Taliesin was aware that Tudlwysti, Brochwel's mother, was still alive, the saintly Queen and patron of saints. This stabbed Brochwel's heart, caught between his father's sword and his mother's heart, neither of which gave way. Both belonged to him. Both were him.

Brochwel's lament was far more than just sorrow. It was impasse, war between a father's warrior destiny and a mother's heart of peace. It drove him, not to violence, but to desperation that totally shook him to the core. Brochwel broke within, and awoke beyond, quite where, he could not say. Brochwel's lament was silent, being neither war nor peace. His father's wars, his mother's peace, both were present in his son and him, and so he came to Merlin, to sit in silence, beyond war or peace.

Merlin welcomed him and went with him to the wisdom cell. Brochwel opened his heart to him, and Merlin listened. No advice, no answers, no neat solutions were appropriate, as two broken souls found wholesome comfort in each other's company.

Brochwel realized Merlin's peace was not peace as this world knows peace, nor peace opposed to it. It was nothing like anything he knew, and yet he knew, and knew he knew, this peace was true. Brochwel's lament had transmuted him, but into what, he could not say.

Brochwel became a life-long friend of Merlin from that hour. Through Merlin, he entered timeless Camelot, deep in his heart, but knew not how. He became a knight of Camelot, though what Camelot was, he could not say. Merlin had told him that Camelot was the name for wherever Arthur's knights abode, wherever

Arthur reigned and dined at the Round Table, and when Arthur moved, Camelot moved.

He knew Camulos, Britain's ancient God of war, gave his name to many citadels, like Camulodunum, the British city on the eastern coast, Rome's Chester on the Cole, called Colchester by Saxons, ensuring British coastal access to lands across the sea. Here, Camelot drove a lasting British wedge between South Anglian folk and East Saxons, confined in turn by the Thames and Jutes in Kent to the south. He knew Camelot was not defined by this but moved, when Arthur moved, present whenever defeat turned to victory, and glory was breaking through. Cadbury and Caerleon were Camelot, too, where Camulos dwelt, leaving many traces in the landscape that spoke of Arthur's holy war.

A castle west of Pengwern was Camelot for a time, Hen Domen, for it commanded the Camlad fords of the Gwern at Rhydwhiman. It was linked to the citadel of Gaer Fawr to the north, commanding the vales of Camlad and the Rea, and Caersws in the west, guarding the upper pasturelands of Gwern.

East of Hen Domen, Caer Guricon, white city on the Gwern, was Camelot once, from where Brochwel now ruled Pengwern. He had learned this from his father, Cyngen. Caer Guricon was Camelot, when Arthur met Merlin here, long ago. Brochwel knew that Arthur once defended Caer Guricon from Saxon Mercians invading from the east. He knew Viroconium had been well known to Merlin since he was with Arthur here, and now it offered peace, with Brochwel's blessing, for Merlin and his five companions on Manstone Mynd.

Camelot left its name in different places that were Arthur's Camelot for a time, and Merlin remembered them all. People would see him go to Camelot to see the king, whenever Arthur needed him. But that was just how it looked on the surface. Camelot would come to him whenever Camulos found a dwelling place, as now, in Brochwel's broken heart. The God of war was delving down to lasting peace, beyond war or peace.

In his extremity, Merlin's wisdom cell offered refuge to Brochwel, for here he could be himself in Camelot, and somehow embrace the warring factions within himself, without false peace. Here Brochwel's lament became his unspoken wisdom song, beneath the tors of Manstone Mynd.

## 22

## MERLIN'S REMEMBERING

Merlin remembered the little things and so kept faith with wisdom. He did not waver, though sometimes wavering arose in him for a while, then passed away. He loved wisdom, whose inspiration, although uncreated, creates and recreates anew in every moment. He wedded wisdom long ago, and loved her dancing creativity, her creative play with images. They gave beauty to light that served the Grail, and form to glory the Grail served. Now that he was old, he saw wisdom interweave his life with her remembering.

Merlin watched over Nimue's wondrous wisdom dance within the Throne, as she passed through earth to stone, from stone to fathomless waters deep beneath fissured quartzite crags. He loved to watch her descending down into the lake, opening caverns, where at the nether end the lake was fire, soaring way beyond the tors as starlit sky. He loved her descending embrace, as air was fire and flame consumed him. He became her flame, distilled and cooled into healing waters, nourishing springs to hallow and renew the land.

Merlin watched as wisdom danced among the shimmering stars and burst into bright flame, burying herself in bluestone calm to cure the dolorous wound. He saw, through her clarity, insight that buried stars in bluestone tombs.

Was it foresight or farsight, this vision that saw glory in a grain of sand, and heaven in a wild flower? Was it light that saw glory in a hazelnut, resting in the palm of his hand? Was it prophecy or predictions that wisdom loved, wonder or miracles that worked her glorious deeds? He steadied at the brink of time and held critical tension taut, Pendragon union of wedded dragons that do not fly apart. Wisdom loved is wisdom known, wisdom recognized and welcomed home.

Merlin Silvaticus withdrew to the wolds, a wild green man in the forest wilderness, and his life of vision stones and riven rings was wed to wisdom. It was not his power of prediction, but ringed insight beneath the tors that prophesied. Taliesin knew this and treasured it, because it inspired his heart with wisdom song. He loved the wisdom in Merlin's wild dance, and it was wisdom, not magic powers, that inspired him.

Taliesin mused as Merlin's life unfolded such deep remembering. He let reciprocal remembrance remember him, as wisdom revealed in Merlin what had inspired him. Some tales tell that Merlin had been King Myrddin in Carmarthen, before the battle that shattered and illumined him. Three brothers died, sons of Peredur, prince and ally in the north. Three brothers lay buried under stone, waiting to be raised. Merlin mourned and Taliesin mourned with him.

The wilds claimed Merlin and made him wild. Wisdom deranged him before she made him whole. Derangement undid him to remake him, as light turned him outside in, and glory turned him inside out. Like a war-shocked veteran, he slept rough beneath the trees. He hid in caves, and wandered wild in trackless woods. Abiding high in ancient hills, he slept under shooting stars on mountain tors. He met the horned Lord of the wilds, and imbibed the wisdom of the Elder Hunt. Winter closed in round him and shut him out of hold and home. He almost died when winter starved him, and his friend the wolf did die of cold.

Merlin was seated alone by a mountain spring when Ganieda found him and took him in. The bluebells flowered and a sister's love was music to his soul, music from the seven spheres that healed and hallowed him. Merlin awoke as wisdom entered him.

Just as Merlin the child fathered Merlin the prophet-king, so Merlin the mage fathered Merlin, sage and seer. Merlin died a threefold death, the deaths of Lailoken that transformed him. He fell, he hung, he drowned. Merlin fell away from himself as others saw him, hung upside down in wisdom's expanse, and drowned in wisdom's waters that regenerated him. Taliesin lived in song his triple death with him.

His threefold death made Merlin's wife a baffled widow, and he a seer whose crystal cave was like a celestial observatory. In it, he beheld the stars and discerned the spiralling circles of their wisdom dance. Merlin saw in vision seventy windows and

128

seventy doors, and seventy fay scribes recording the movements that informed the cosmic dance. Taliesin watched with Merlin and saw with him what he saw.

Rhydderch died and Ganieda left the Cumbrian court, to extract with Merlin healing remedies from the fires of dragon powers. Were dragons warring or wedding? Were opposing winds at war, or dancing? Were the elements at war or were the seasons wed with elemental love? Merlin studied natural things to read the sacred land. Taliesin studied myths of old to reinterpret sacred times.

When Merlin saw dragon wars as dragons wed in crystal caves beneath the Throne, he traced Pendragon union to its source upstream from Arthur's court and Galahad's return. He held the Hermetic staff of dragons intertwined, and whatever he touched began to heal through them. His work beneath the Throne restored light to sovereign glory in the dragon's heart.

Remembering was Merlin's wisdom work, now that loves and wars were over and his sight grew dim. Remembering was Taliesin's wisdom work, turning Merlin's remembrance into wisdom song, renewing the tradition of the bards. The union of seer and bard healed dolorous wounds and hallowed the land.

Pendragon wisdom purified rings of power seduced by dark sorcery in age after age. It forged rings of wisdom in rings of fire, employing furnaces that only fay smiths and alchemists in nether worlds can master. Rings take shape again and again, as strange chance invites swords and stones to return. Merlin recognized them and Taliesin sang of them. Pendragon wisdom, loved and known again, broke out in song. The Red Ring of Fire and the White Ring of Light opened radiant light to dazzling glory, beneath Black Dragon Tors on Manstone Mynd.

# 23

# RHAEADER, ELIJAH AND TALIESIN

It was in late autumn that Rhaeader arrived from his hermitage, the Llan that bears his name, beneath the Berwyn Falls. He came south to consult Taliesin, friend and fellow bard, for both were graduates of the School of Bards on Cadair Idris.

Since those far-off days, Rhaeader had met Gildas and was convinced by him. He left court to live alone above the Tanat Vale, and often withdrew to the Bowl of the Bards beneath the falls. There and at Llyn Luncaws, on the moor of graves, he met Elijah on the Throne of Cadair Berwyn and remembered that Taliesin had said Merlin encountered Enoch on the Throne of Manstone Mynd.

Rhaeader told Taliesin that he heard a still small voice, gently whispering: 'I am 'I AM,' thy God. This is my Name, and I do not give glory to another. Turn and see! 'I AM' in the midst of thee.'

The Berwyn burned, and Rhaeader saw Elijah rise, for he saw Berwyn to be Sinai here, just as Horeb was Sinai in the east. Suddenly, as he turned to see, the Throne grew wings and soared. Seven heavens opened as seven hells rose, uniting hells with heavens in netherworlds of glorious kings. He mounted the winged chariot throne, but Elijah held the reins, whilst Rhaeader rode uncharted stars. He knew the winged throne of Idris, but had been unfamiliar with the wisdom of the Name. Taliesin assured him all was well, and that the Serpent's Pool would confirm the whisper of the still small voice. It would send ripples from the deeps at centre, right to him. The Chair of Berwyn would confirm it too, when the mists arose to unveil the glory of the Name.

Rhaeader saw the shimmering ripples of the pool pass from its depths to his feet, and the clouds rose to reveal the Name. But in the Cauldron of the Bards, as the falls froze, he saw messengers of ice appear among the stones, and wondered what they meant. Was it that Idris was present in the revelation of the Man, and was Gwyn blessing the unveiling of the Name? Idris was guardian of the lore of bards, and held seals to the wisdom Chair. Was Rhaeader deserting him by his way of life in the Llan, or was Idris gracing him by sending angels of ice at the falls?

Taliesin had asked such questions many times, for, like Rhaeader, he too was an Idris bard, and owed allegiance to the lineage of the Cauldron and the Chair. Taliesin had put these matters to the test, and over many years had found the lineage of Elijah to confirm and complete the lineage of Idris. For bards, Idris was the test, and Elijah confirmed him. For the Temple in Old Jerusalem, the Name was the test, and Taliesin knew that in the east, Idries was Enoch's name, in Arabic.

Taliesin told Rhaeader of Name and Throne on Manstone Mynd, the mystery of turning, seeing and being seen. He told

Rhaeader of Nialfingal, King of Barra in the Outer Isles, which some called the Hebrides, whose castle in the bay was safe haven to all seeking refuge from raging seas. Nialfingal had sought the Grail and found the Name. He asked if this 'I AM' was the One, or ought he to look for another? On Ben Rulibrec in Vatersay, he heard: 'I am 'I AM,' all yea, no nay, all glory, so be it, as it is.' This answered Nialfingal's question and unveiled the Secret of the Grail. He did not look for another.

Taliesin spoke with Merlin of Rhaeader's quest, and together they went with him, by way of the Eye, to the Throne on Manstone Mynd. There, they invoked Idris in the presence of the Man, and questioned the Man Stone with regard to the Gwyn Stone by the Berwyn Throne.

Who was king, or were there many kings? Who held the keys, and whose graves were these? Who broke the seals, and opened revelation in the nether pools? Who guarded the entrance to other worlds? Was it Gwyn or Idris, Elijah or the Man who reigned on Manstone Mynd?

Then, as Merlin gazed, Idris appeared upon the Throne and pointed to Gwyn, who pointed to the Man that Enoch saw to be the Son of Man, seer when seeing sees. Then, Cadair the Chair became the Throne and unveiled the Name in every name, assuring the bard that his myth was true.

The netherworld was not hell, but a world of fay, of mystery and of wonder. It was a kingdom of wondrous light, in whose light, light wrought rings of light from light. Gwyn's stone was the Man's Stone without division, because here Man was not opposed, does not oppose. He reigns as light in his Kingdom of Light, saying: 'Turn and see, the Kingdom is here.' Netherworlds are present, and everywhere the ring quest is fulfilled.

Rhaeader listened and heard the gentle whisper that Elijah heard, and Taliesin blessed his life beneath the Berwyn Falls. Rhaeader returned, and whenever he could, withdrew to listen to the voices in the waters of the Cauldron, and read the message in the angel's ice. Sometimes, the Berwyn Pool was still, and sometimes the centre stirred, and cast forth ripples that spoke of so much more than words could tell. Sometimes, Gwyn, the King of the Netherworld, would stir, as the stone that bears his name would move, thrum and dance among the graves.

Then elders of the Elder Days would dance, and join the waters of Rhaea as she plunged from the heights into her pools, each cascade an elemental expression of Lady Rhaea's wisdom falls. Rhaeader knew his name simply meant, Rhaea's falls, and was glad both giant and giantess beside his cell had blessed his coming and remaining there. He never forgot that the fay bridge beneath the arch led to the netherworld, and Gwyn, its king, was blessing him to guard the cauldron of the falls.

Rhaeader treasured the wisdom transmitted by Merlin and Taliesin, seer and bard. For him, the war of pagan rings was over, now that warring rings were transfixed by fire, and anchored in light by the Rood. The Ringed Rood freed rings of power from

Odin's Age of Iron, and showed Wotan that whilst a will to power may coerce, rings of fire flame free. Merlin's rings of wisdom did not dominate, or have a will of their own. They did not subject the bearer to their power, but opened hearts to wisdom.

Rhaeader tended the Druid's Bowl as a transforming Grail. He welcomed Rhaea's falls and turned them into gentle, healing streams and cooling pools. Here, by Berwyn's Throne, wisdom streams were renewing the land, transforming into healing rings of peace the warring rings of Bronze and Iron.

# 24

## SHROUD OF EDESSA.

On Avalon, isle of remembrance, Seraph Nasciens became blind, blinded by the light that serves the Grail. Seraph was an Arimathean of Joseph's line, whose father cared for Joseph's Holy Shroud in Edessa. Mar Thoma's twin had sent the shroud with him, his twin, to Edessa, to heal Abgar, its king. In the Cathedral Church of Holy Wisdom, it was called the Mandylion, doubled in four, for the Shroud was folded into eight, leaving visible only the face, the holy icon not made with hands.

Seraph was old, and withdrew to Archangel Llan in Dysynny Dale, and cried vision down on Bird Rock Tor. The shoreline hugged the rock-face scree, giving cormorants sheltered nesting grounds among the crags. Dysynny seers put seeing first, becoming the mystery that seeing sees. As a disciple of Druid seers, Seraph had acquired their skills, but nothing had prepared him for the glory of the Grail. It blinded him: not the chalice as such, but the glory that the thanksgiving feast revealed and veiled. He was not ready then, but now had spent a lifetime attuning his perception, opening his heart to light.

As a boy, Seraph had seen the Shroud in the Cathedral Church of Edessa, and was shown the Vision Stone that guarded hallows in the Sanctuary of Holy Wisdom. Joseph's Shroud bore the image not made with hands that veiled the face of glory of the risen one. It was a veil that veiled the glory of resurrection, lest it blind him with its dazzling light. Though veiled to curious scrutiny, it preserved the image to unveil glory to those with eyes to see.

Seraph saw not only the facial form on linen, but the formless glory it unveiled. Thus it was that when Seraph saw the Grail, shrouded in mist in Avalon, he saw the glory it veiled too. It blinded him, but his heart could see, for it was awake.

Seraph sought Nimue in Goatshaw Ring, to discover healing for his sight, unveiled by revelation of the Name. She told him why the unveiled face required a veil to be unveiled, leaving an image not made by human hands. She reminded him that Avalon veils the glory of resurrection, lest it blind us with its light. She said that Avalon also lifts the veil aside, to ensure it does not obscure what it unveils.

Nimue took Seraph to Oak Hill on the west side of the Mynd, where the stronghold of Castle Ring held firm, encircled by precipitous cliffs and vallum banks. Cavernous dingles surrounded the ancient Ring, each ruled by dragon powers, the Dingle of Ragon the Red, and the Dingle of Agon the White.

Nimue showed Seraph how the dragons bled their energies into steep banks, and made the cliffs impregnable. Here, since elder days, the moot was held that called for Pendragon vision in Pengwern Lands. Here, Nimue opened Seraph's eyes with energies from the bleeding Lance, eyes blinded by the glory of the

Grail. Longinus had given his Lance to Joseph, who bequeathed it with the Grail to the Fisher King at Carbonek. Its energies served the glory of the Grail and so were sustaining Nimue, watched over by the Eye of Solomon's Ring. Conjoining light to glory, Seraph's eyes were healed, and his heart sustained steady seeing until his dying day. Ageless Nimue imparted light, the light Seraph saw with the eyes of his heart. Blindness was mere sleep to him, waking his heart to vision.

Nimue told Seraph that Avalon veiled vision until hearts were ready, renewing wisdom in nine spheres, each ruled by a seer of Avalon's all-seeing Lake. She told him she was one of the Nine, and that all Nine were endowed with healing rings. Morgana the Fay and two nether seers tended Arthur there, shrouded from sight, alight with insight. That is why the myth tells of Arthur's coming again when needed, as Pendragon's once and future king. The veil conceals, the shroud unveils what eye sees not and hearts reveal.

Nimue returned with Seraph to Manstone Mynd. She showed Seraph the four cascading pools beneath the Throne that veil the elemental fires of air, earth, water and fire. Air's limpid awareness, earth's grounding stillness, water's intuitive vision and fire's burning love imparted the Hermetic arts of sacred alchemy, which she explained were venom cures for poisoned wounds. Poison, extracted from dragons, fed remedies to heal the dolorous wound.

The Lake of healing was a sea of kindly remembrance, making all things new. In wisdom, the translucent gaze and kiss embraced. When waters rose, mists descended, veiling dragons and fay powers. When wisdom returns, Pendragon energies reveal what Avalon concealed.

Nimue had hidden access, through Merlin's union of stars and stones, to four hallows, the Shroud, the Lance, the Grail, and the Ring. She transmitted the healing energies of all four hallows to Seraph Nasciens in Goatshaw Ring.

The Shroud was glory unveiled as a face in repose. The Lance transformed blind Seraph, healing his sight when glory hallowed his heart. The Grail veiled and unveiled glory, whose light kept powers at bay. The Ring brought healing to all who suffered under rings of power. Merlin presided over Pendragon smiths and alchemists in netherworlds, generating healing rings anew.

Avalon and Edessa concealed hallows that harrowed hells. Shroud, Lance, Grail and Ring furrowed hearts to plant and harvest wisdom. They restored the land, remembering a once and future Davidic king. Solomon's Ring was stolen by Asmodeus when its keeper was heedless, so Nimue was watchful, lest hallows were stolen and their virtues usurped by warring extremes. Nimue tended the four hallows, healing all who were imbibing Pendragon wisdom, on the slopes of Manstone Mynd.

# 25

# FISSURE FOLD

Merlin sometimes walked along Manstone Mynd to the crevice, and sat within the stone circle of Fissure Fold. Listening to the stones, he had long ago been made aware of the great fault and its ruptures beneath the waters of the hidden Lake. But although he could sense where volatile faults split or fused, he could not work with them here on the surface. He had to go home beneath the Throne, if he was to do wisdom work in the crystal cave with that which unveiled itself at Fissure Fold.

Merlin returned along the Mynd, and slowly ascended the Throne. Passing through the Needle's Eye to the crystal cave beneath the Throne, he saw where powers beneath upheld the Man enthroned, but some, resisting, were resisted. It was not a mere place in space or a moment in time, but an ancient cleft, a crack of doom, a split among primordial powers. It was a Cherubic Throne that took flawed energies and transformed them into a footstool of quartz crags.

Ascenders spoke of angels, good and bad, but descenders scoffed, dismissive of myths and impatient with energy they could not control. Both were vulnerable, as Merlin knew, for ascenders, if driven by fear, saw dark powers everywhere, and descenders, driven by ignorance, saw only what their senses saw. Sometimes, both were like children, who played with fractured powers without realizing the powers were playing with them. Near the great fault, they could unleash dissipating energies with naïve abandon, oblivious to what was controlling them. Both ascent and descent were capable of spreading viral ruptures, parasitic and poisonous, unaware they were toxic, deadly to all.

Taliesin knew the myth itself, ascent and descent, was originally a power to heal. But in the hands of fear, it could be a power insinuating fear. In the hands of ignorance, it could be a power instilling ignorance, for even when ignorance was in denial of myth, it was still, though unaware, driven by incoherent myth.

Merlin saw the roots of fear and ignorance lurking deep beneath the Throne, for the crystal cave held many secrets that were not accessible above. The outer senses handled the surfaces of things, but were not seeing what seers see and wisdom frees to be. Landscape was blind until inscape unveiled inklings of dragon mysteries within the tors.

Merlin in the crystal cave undertook the work of discerning what fear and ignorance overlooked. He delved beneath the Throne, to unravel twisted dragons that surfaced at Fissure Fold. He worked with Taliesin to free the myth from its enslavement to fear and ignorance. He worked with Nimue to free sovereignty from confusion and dominion from division, and transform the dull lead of airy fear and stony ignorance into red-gold wisdom rings.

Incoherence festered down here, and ambivalence resisted sound union at all cost. But where was its root? Where did the roots of confusion and division lie? In the crystal cave, Merlin could see symptoms but not the root, so he plunged down into the Lake, and followed hidden faults to where fissures emerged on surfaces elsewhere. He searched beneath Fissure Fold, but to no avail. He had never managed to discover there where the roots emerged.

So Merlin listened to the wisdom of the Throne, and found that the Lake concealed the great split, and countless fissures too. He saw fear's ascending root emerge from the depths of a great fault on Glastonbury Tor, whilst the descending root of ignorance emerged from rifts far under Silbury Hill. Both sites were sanctuaries of great power, so Merlin decided that he would go and see what was happening to fear on Glastonbury Tor, and how ignorance was leaking out on Silbury Hill.

On Glastonbury Tor, he saw fear slide down to Avalon, where veils closed in round fear and held it in, without cure. At Silbury Hill, he saw ignorance leak out and spread throughout the land. The key to a cure, the waters told him, was Avebury Ring, which Merlin knew was an axial hub. The energies there were allied with healing powers across the plain in the Bluestone Ring of the Great Henge. Both were wholesome, but fear and ignorance were far too primitive to co-operate with them.

The leak was catastrophic on Silbury Hill, for it was there that knowledge was confused with ignorance, leaking ignorance everywhere. On the surface, rings of blessing were being confused with rings of power, so that the great divide beneath imposed itself above. Silbury Hill was still a place of great power, but neglect had made it vulnerable to invasion by contagious ignorance. It was so old that the roots of knowledge there had been forgotten.

Merlin invoked the Man, King of Manstone Mynd, and Gwyn came too, with Enoch, working together to seek out fissures of the fault, and call them to account. The Man Stone and the Gwyn Stone moved, and their spirits woke, stirring as one with Enoch. As if moving to a silent dance, they wove golden rings round warring powers, undoing their cunning rule in the deeps. Some released, but some resisted, and Merlin realized the root of fear and ignorance lay here.

He watched as Enoch danced, one with the Man, or Son of Man, curing fissured powers of obsessions that led to war, claiming sovereignty beneath the Throne. It was not long before immense energies gathered and began to dance to a different rhythm, as light transformed them in the midst. They agreed to acknowledge a greater glory than the breached power they used to serve. They began to chant a Cherubic Hymn upholding a Cherubic Throne, now that the Man was present and his chant was danced.

Wisdom chant began to enchant fear, weaving ascending haloes with descending crowns. The dance of rings turned fear outside in and ignorance inside out, whilst descending stars were embedded in ascending stones. The chant danced on, inspiring fear to transcend fear and ignorance to embrace wisdom, even as wisdom ascended and glory descended to heal the land.

Merlin led the dancing chant through Avebury Ring to West Kennet Way, where paired dragon stones closed the leak of fear in Glastonbury, and absorbed ignorance back into encircling wisdom rings within Silbury Hill. Pendragon pairs enclosed the powers and sealed the disastrous leak. Red and white dragons conjoined to heal the world, freeing Pendragon wisdom to shine again beneath the stars.

Ignorance was cured as Merlin led the dance along fissured chasms from Avalon to Glastonbury, embracing fear and ignorance. Fear was terrified, but came with him, caught up in the rhythm of the dance. Ignorance was confused but hesitantly willing to see if ascent could shed its disastrous stress, by releasing strain through wise, not ignorant, descent.

Merlin brought the dance of Avalon round from Glastonbury Tor to Silbury Hill, then to the Great Ring of Avebury itself, Moot of the Great Dance in elder days, and hub of older dances still. The chant danced its way over the great plain to the Healing Henge, where the bluestone ring danced within chanting sarsen giants, imparting healing to the land.

When Merlin led the dance from Avebury Ring to the Bluestone Ring in the Healing Henge, he called forth bluestone energies there, which stirred the parent stones in the Preseli Hills, who gladly joined the dance. This called forth the Great Dance, the dance of stones with stars among the hills, restoring wise sovereignty beneath the Throne, imparting wholeness to the land. It awoke nine stewards of the Lake, who joined with fair bearers of nine fay rings, chanting a dance to heal the fissured roots, the healing dance of Avalon.

Here the dance of stones joined the dance of stars, and the greater dance of suns and galaxies, of cosmic dust and exploding giants. As above, so below, the dance of Merlin wove healing wholeness as he danced. The fissure beneath Glastonbury Tor was sealed and fear released. The leak on Silbury Hill was sealed and ignorance healed.

Merlin's dance became a cherubic dance of translucent stars and healing stones, as light of heaven above wove in and out of peace on earth below. Ringed ascent cured fear and ringed descent cured ignorance, uniting both at centre, where fissures crossed the luminous wisdom axis of the Throne.

The Pendragon dance of dragons beneath the Throne wove peace where fault-line wars dissolved in rings of fire. Fires of dragon breath forged rings of light from rings of power. Wisdom's embrace in the deeps united the gaze of stars and stones with a kiss. As the Nine danced, rings of power transformed into wisdom rings of Pendragon light and fire. The dance of Merlin and the Nine healed the great fault, where rings of fire refined rings of power into rings of light and glory.

Nearer home, Merlin brought the dance back to Fissure Fold, and round to the crystal caves far down below, and lower still to the fathomless depths of the great fault. From there he rose to encircle the stones and castle tors before alighting at centre in Goatshaw Ring. Here, Merlin danced the gnomic chant of Wisdom Wyrd, round a central fire as in the elder days. Then he chanted the Ringed Rood, which wove Barrow elder's wisdom with the Name, uniting old rings with the Rood.

The myth had been remade many times before, for its retelling was an unbroken weave. To the east, Mercians sang of Balder, son of Odin, whose Grail they knew, but Britons sang of the doom of dark powers at the foot of the Gnomic Rood. Wisdom was reweaving the myth of powers beneath the Lake, uniting them under the sovereignty of Rood and Throne.

When Merlin returned to Fissure Fold, he sensed the change in the depths of the stones. Fear receded as ignorance retreated, uniting ringed Wyrd with the Rood. Wisdom's dance was opening hells beneath into heavens of light. Fears dissolved as ignorance was transmuted into wisdom.

Fissure Stones sang wisdom songs and Merlin could hear their resonance among the stars. Wisdom forged Pendragon rings in primordial fires, to heal deep rifts at the root. Merlin was transforming dragon's venom into gentle cures to renew the earth. Wisdom rode dragon's breath as it was curing dolorous wounds. The Ringed Rood wrought great peace, as stars wed stones, on the Throne of Manstone Mynd.

# 26

## SEERS OF THE GRAIL

Galahad, seer of the Grail, had grown in wisdom and stature, inspired by Dindrane's heart of knowing love. Nurturing him in insight and wonder, she imparted to him the Name, whose origin is only known by awakening to wisdom. Galahad saw the Grail and the tors of the wasteland shimmer with glory. He discerned Pendragon wisdom in dancing stones and summer stars. Galahad saw the Grail, but it was his heart that saw its light, and his spirit that knew its glory.

In ruined Britain, stars and stones had been at war. In the wasteland, ascent was ruled by fear, and descent was ruled by ignorance. Ascent ended in ignominious fall and descent led disintegration into ignorance, and there was no remedy, as long as the cure and the ruin were at war with themselves.

The British were losing the Battle for Britain because Britain was at war with peace and cut off from healing. Galahad's quest was tearing Pendragon union apart, shattering what wisdom unites. Galahad learned from experience that ascent alone, driven by fear, was not the cure. He learned that Merlin's wisdom was Pendragon descent wed with balanced ascent, and that Dindrane's Arimathean heart of love was true.

Merlin was seer of the Grail, not by interfering in the life of kings, but by leading the dance of wisdom down into ruptured depths, and dancing wisdom's dance with fissured powers. Rings of power were remade as rings of wisdom. Rings of healing rose from the roots of the Throne, restoring sovereignty between the hills. Merlin's alchemy transformed rings of power with rings of fire, forging rings of peace sealed by stones and stars.

Merlin the prophet-sage was seer of Grail mysteries that healed lethal rings by chanting the Pendragon dance of stars and stones. Taliesin was seer of the Grail, not as poetic celebrity, but as bard whose wisdom restored the myth. Nimue was seer of the Grail, by trusting wisdom to see as seeing sees, and remembering the little things. Dindrane was seer of the Grail, not by exclusion but by communion, union embracing the other in her heart of love. Ganieda was seer of the Grail, not as a sorrowing widowed Queen, but as gentle seer, whose prophecy transmitted wisdom, welcomed home by prayer. Maeldin was seer of the Grail, not by advocating healing springs, but by being the healing spring so that wisdom sings.

Seers of the Grail were no longer obsessed with a Grail out there, so sophists no longer scoffed at seeking seers. They turned from sophistry to wisdom, loving wisdom that sustained seeing as the Grail sees. Merlin's seers rose from light to light, in ascent, and kept the seeing, from glory to glory, in descent. Trusting the seeing, they remembered little things, which meant they excluded nothing from wisdom's embrace of gaze and kiss. The wisdom of

148

Mary Magdala was remembered. The wisdom of Joseph of Arimathea unveiled the Holy of Holies, a Bridal Chamber at the heart of Solomon's Cherubic Throne.

Merlin transmitted integral wisdom in the Name of names. The question: 'Who serves the Grail?' was answered by awakening to ascending light. The question: 'Whom does the Grail serve?' imparted descending glory, embracing all things in wisdom that ascent excludes. Both questions were crucial, for the Ring serves whoever really serves the Ring. The questions consumed themselves like tail-eating dragons. Merlin knew that the wisdoms of Mar Thoma and of Mary Magdala were both twinned to the wisdom of Yeshuah their Twin, whose heart lies hidden in the secrets of Grail and Ring.

Galahad made no claim to be wise, but trusted instead in wisdom. The seat of peril was not dangerous to wisdom but to the blind who claimed to be wise, refusing to surrender their divided minds and confused hearts. Elaine had given her life to give birth to Galahad, and when she died, Dindrane was like a mother to him. Dindrane's heart of love mothered wisdom, inspiring him beyond ascent, to embrace descent.

Neither Druid Oak nor Healing Henge had been so explicit. The hexagram was David's Star because as above, so below, ascent embraces wise descent with a kiss. The pentagram was Solomon's Star because wisdom's gaze was endless. Like the dragon consuming itself by the tail, it embraced everything. As mystic symbol of eternity, the Name swallowed past and future, leaving sapphire seals on red-gold rings. In wise indwelling, we die each other's life and live each other's death, the Matter of Byzantium. The Matter of Britain was peace, as love and wisdom know.

Joseph of Arimathea rejoiced at Galahad's ascent, but was sore amazed at Merlin's descent, struck dumb to see the Grail was seer as well as seen. Joseph of Nazareth rejoiced that his son's spiritual twin was Sage in India, with Arimathean Guardians, heirs in Malabar to Davidic Thrones.

Nicodemus of Jerusalem rejoiced that Merlin transmitted wisdom on Manstone Mynd, and Taliesin renewed bardic myth, in dancing light of stars and stones. Mary Magdala watched over Nimue's embrace of the gaze of stars and the kiss of stones, timeless in her caves in Saint Baume Grotte. She tended the tenderness of Dindrane's heart as she sustained Galahad, and held together in Provence what elsewhere flies apart.

Wisdom united Rood and Ring in Merlin's Britain, bequeathing a Ringed Rood, union of old Druid rings and the Byzantine Cross. Merlin imparted this when he saw Odin's one-eyed wisdom in the light of the wisdom of both twins' single eye. He bequeathed Odin's Ash as a Tree of Life in Solomon's Temple on Jerusalem's Holy Mount. Merlin's re-forging of old rings of power, in a ring of fire, changed the world beneath the Throne. At the crack of doom, Merlin used hell's fires to burn up hell, transforming lead to gold. At the root of the Throne, he forged rings of wisdom that generated gold from gold, granting Pendragon rings to all whose hearts were homes to wisdom.

Wisdom rejoiced at Merlin's hidden circle of turned minds and illumined hearts, waxing strong in Powys and Pengwern. She delighted in the forest seas of Nimue, and the lakes and springs of the Nine. She watched over the waters of remembrance that embraced little things. She inspired the crystal stones beneath the Throne to abide in one another as they purified rings of power. She protected Galahad in the chair of peril, and all who with him die in life to all that fear obscures. Blessing all in all, she crowned the Man in the Stone, who rode the devouring dragon as a Throne, on the tors of Manstone Mynd.

# 27

# TALIESIN AND DINDRANE

Taliesin and Dindrane loved wisdom, and saw wisdom loved and known in Nimue and Merlin. Taliesin renewed the Merlin myth in the sacred tradition of Pendragon bards, and Dindrane renewed wisdom in illumined hearts, in the sacred tradition of hermit saints.

Like Solomon of old, in his Song of Songs, Dindrane took the mysteries of wisdom and through her love of Taliesin lived them as peace. Dindrane chose the path of love for all as her wisdom's glory, embracing all in Taliesin and Taliesin in all. She embraced the wisdom of both Davidic twins as twinned wisdom, light wed to glory, and glory wed to light. Taliesin was glory to her light as she was glory to his light, and all was seen as glory loved and known by light, wherever they turned.

The legacy of Dindrane was Galahad, but Galahad transformed. She knew ascent to light was not enough, for in Britain it had led to catastrophic descent. In her, gentle descent, as well as balanced ascent, were together loved and known. Taliesin's function was to sing wisdom songs of light's love of glory, and glory's love of light, woven into all, through all. It was to give form and image to Dindrane's love, inspired by his love of her, but transmuted from light to glory.

Nothing was left out.  Nothing was despised.  Taliesin held tension taut, for if too slack, the lyre did not resound, and if too tight, it broke.  Critical tension upheld his wisdom song, like a warrior's bow.  Dindrane did not need to understand the critical tension of bards, but loving wisdom in Taliesin, she fulfilled its truth by love.  Co-inherence dissolved incoherence in each of them, and mirrored union to each awakening heart.

The wisdom of Mar Thoma mirrored the wisdom of his twin, and Dindrane took this wisdom and embraced it in him.  Her love for Taliesin awoke wisdom in her heart that had no bounds.  Taliesin worked with images and through her image, saw Dindrane everywhere, loving everyone as he loved her.

The tradition of the wisdom twins was the wisdom of the Holy Three in Sarras.  The legacy of hallowed stones was the wisdom of the Holy Tree.  Lake and spring, oak and henge, were all transmitting waters of light in Avalon.  The wisdom of Prester John mirrored the wisdom of Melchizedek, in Davidic kings that inspired Solomon's heirs in Old Byzantium.

Taliesin wedded Enoch's wisdom with the wisdom of the Healing Henge, the wisdom of ancestral elders and masters of the hunt.  Nothing was too little to be noticed in wisdom song.  Nothing was too lowly to be included in the chant.  Ganieda remembered everything, and Maeldin wrote it down.  No one was left out or excluded from the dance.

Mordred was remembered here, and all who wished them ill. Brochwel was remembered here and all who wished them well. Morgana was loved for who she was, not hated for what she did. Orcs were not forgotten here, remembering they were elves. Wraiths were at peace once more, remembering they were kings. Muggles discovered magic that wizards gladly shared. They treasured hallows that Merlin generously passed on to them. Taliesin gave the myth new life, opening light to glory, as Dindrane took the myth to heart and transmitted it by love.

Taliesin in Byzantium received the Holy Name, and shared its wisdom with all with hearts to see. Dindrane received it as the mystery of the Grail, and found the Grail was receptive to the wisdom of the Name. Grail and Name danced their wedding dance in her through him, as wisdom danced in both their hearts, in him through her.

Taliesin sang of Merlin's peace that Nimue passed on, and Dindrane pondered peace of heart, in which all belong. Harrowing hells in delves below Goatshaw Ring, peace rang out as wisdom song, on the screes of Manstone Mynd.

# 28

# MERLIN AND NIMUE

Merlin's birth had been a mystery, and his death was a mystery too. Indeed, many believed he never really died, or that his death somehow consumed death, raising him. Like Elijah, who ascended in a chariot throne, they thought Merlin arose on the Man Stone's Throne, but not alone. Taliesin and Dindrane, Ganieda and Maeldin were with him, one in spirit, through wisdom and the Name.

Nimue was with him too, receiving from him the wisdom that made her prophet, mage, seer and sage. Some said she fulfilled these functions beyond a normal span of human years. Others said she died, still others that her love for Merlin and his love for her were not subject to death, being an uncreated love, which is not in time. Some say their wisdom's uncreated creativity is still bearing fruit, and that treasures are discovered from time to time that are their gift. These hallows transmit wisdom, light and glory, to heal the land.

The legacy of Merlin was passed on to Nimue, who transmitted Arimathean hallows: Shroud, Lance, Grail and Ring. Nine hallowing wisdom rings watched over holy hallows, transmitting light and glory. Nimue's ring was one of the Nine, and it could unveil the glory the Shroud veiled, and the light that pierced hearts, healing dolorous wounds with a Lance. As Seer of Avalon's Lake of Remembrance, Nimue transmitted the light that serves the Grail, never forgetting the glory the Grail serves.

Nimue had spent years imbibing the mysteries of the King's Great Ring. In the crystal cave beneath the Throne, she was heir to the wisdom of the Healing Henge, but had received, with Solomon's Ring, the wisdom transmission of Byzantium. She was discovering the wisdom of the Ringed Rood, in the light of the older traditions of the Groves of Oak and elders of the Barrow Shrines.

Avalon was heir to Solomon's heirloom Ring as well as Druidic transmission of the lore of kings. Nimue's wisdom work with Merlin freed the Nine from warring powers, and so remade ruined Britain in the sovereign strength of Solomon's Great Ring. The reigning Ring was not a ring that overpowered other rings, but freely empowered them to be what they were meant to be.

Known in the east as the Ring of Solomon the King, it was known by other names to Merlin. There were old tales of Solomon's Ring, but most thought it had been lost, or that it was only a figment of the imagination of poets or bards. It was a Ring that grounded the embrace of glory in primordial wisdom, giving light to awakened hearts.

The Druids had known of wisdom rings long before the reign of Solomon, but once wisdom was exiled from the Temple in

Jerusalem, the King's Ring had passed by way of the Order of Melchizedek, an unbroken line of Davidic seers, to Mar Thoma's twin. From him, it passed to the Arimatheans in Jerusalem, and from them to Avalon, wisdom's new home in the Isles.

The energy of Solomon's Ring had passed to Nimue, after Merlin's work with warring dragons beneath the tors was done. Imagined wars had conditioned love to end in war. Now love's embrace of red and white, beneath the veil, stripped black tors of darkness, revealing light in the quartz. Wedded dragons concealed love's glory in caves beneath the mines.

Merlin passed on to Nimue the arts of alchemy and a refining fire that worked with dragon's energies in ancient mines. Fay wrights and alchemists wrought swords and torques, crowns and rings, which still retained their hallowing energy. The Mynd was a maze of hidden mines that led into other worlds and long-forgotten times.

Nimue had learned to read the Seeing Stones that gave access to all hallowed treasures, opening seers to the inmost heart of hallows and fay hallowing. She had imbibed Merlin's insight into fallen kings, who imposed their will to power on all whom they deceived. Their dark magic insinuated itself into scrolls and weapons, jewels and crowns, once their bearers were slaves to its cruel power. It was undone down here, by dragon fire, in the deepest mines.

But wisdom's work is never done, and Merlin's mantle, together with Solomon's Ring, was passed on from Nimue and the Nine. Her work embraced his, but extended it to include the mysteries of the Lake, bringing deep healing by way of wise remembrance. This enabled her, in caves of light, to address the traumas of Morgana and Morgause, half-sisters of Arthur, seers of Avalon.

Morgana could not heal Arthur, because her own wounds went too deep. When he passed into the shadows, she became a shadow of herself. When Nimue entered the Cave of Light and welcomed Morgana there, her heart awoke and wept. Sclerosis melts like ice in spring when light warms hearts with uncreated fire. The frozen fissures deep in Morgana's heart were healed, curing Morgause, and Arthur too.

Nimue's wisdom work was hidden, and only hints of it were passed on, except in circles that were close to Merlin. Manstone Mynd was overlooked, enclosed by the forests of Pengwern, and the mysteries of its ancient mines were forgotten, except by Nimue's heirs and Taliesin's bards. Inklings of wisdom remain obscure, until the day of wisdom's return.

When Merlin discovered the Cave of Light, he shared its mysteries with Nimue beyond the deepest shafts. Old Roman mines had bored into dark regions of hidden springs, opening out into luminous streams that watered nether worlds. Caverns beneath black dragon tors led to a Cave of Light, where Merlin showed Nimue how to unveil obscurity above to reveal bright clarity below. Here, he unravelled knots that had led to Arthur's demise, but it was Nimue's task to heal the Nine in Avalon. Nimue's luminous heart, in the strength of Solomon's Ring, embraced those hells, welcoming Morgana back. Mending her broken soul, the Great Ring purified the rings of the Nine, by refining them in rings of fire. It consumed power by fire, releasing translucent energy.

Other hallows came from the Lake, but they often remained unrecognized. It was the function of Davidic kings and Stewards of the Lake to recognize what was so often overlooked. Both Lance and Shroud came from Joseph, the Lance transmitting ascending light, the Shroud imparting resurrection glory. Arimatheans did not concern themselves with physical bloodlines of earthly kings, knowing that it was the transmission of wisdom that would discern the Secret of the Grail, and open the mysteries that the Grail served.

Nimue, as Lady of the Lake, received Excalibur, returned to her by Bedivere at Arthur's behest. But Excalibur returns as a two-edged sword whenever incoherence, due to confusion, separating stars and stones, threatens to usurp co-inherence.

Solomon's Ring, bearing the Name and Star, still imparts the music of the spheres. It generates rings that teach the language of stones and stars, haloes in rings of purifying fire. Hallows still illumine their bearers so that they discern dragon's breath in quartzite tors and dragon's blood in rings of fire.

Tales of Merlin on Manstone Mynd point beyond themselves to the Matter of Britain. Whenever Britain is in danger of falling apart, the wisdom of Merlin is there to make peace. The older wisdom, conjoined with the wisdom of Byzantium, discerns roods in rings and stars in stones. It wends its way, in later times, to Cistercian scribes and Troubadour minstrels in France, inspiring Minnesingers in Germany, eventually to embrace the world.

It was wisdom that mattered to Merlin, for whom Britain was most herself when her love of wisdom was widely loved and known. Merlin shared this legacy of wisdom with Nimue, who wedded wisdom with him. Both transmit wisdom as light from light, in age after age, as unspent mysteries of glory in rings of the Rood. Their love was a love of wisdom, which saw in the other the wisdom they both loved. This mutual mirroring is present still in all, who like them, love wisdom.

There is no end to the mysteries of the Matter of Britain, embracing English, Irish, Scot and Pict, with Briton and Breton in rings of fire. Nor are there limits to the Matter of Byzantium, awakening the light that serves the Grail, and transmitting the glory the Grail serves. The once and future king is as timeless as the dance of the Man on the Throne. He heals fissures and great faults, wedding stars and stones.

The tales of Merlin and Nimue on Manstone Mynd appeared to end long ago, but in the legacy of Taliesin and the bards, of

Dindrane and the works of love, they never end. Light loves glory in the mirror of the Name, and glory loves light as radiance of wisdom. In every age, Merlin and Nimue impart wisdom in their love, and love in their wisdom. Taliesin, inspired by Dindrane, transmits wisdom songs to all, even to this day.

The work of Merlin opens Avalon mysteries of the Lake in every age. As ringed wisdom, wedding stars and stones in quartzite tors, the work of bards regenerates the myth, to renew vision in questing souls. Taliesin and Dindrane, Ganieda and Maeldin, heal minds and hearts far beyond the boundaries of Goatshaw Ring. With Nimue and Merlin, they transmit light that serves the Grail, and glory the Grail serves, witnessing dragons red and white, beneath the Throne. There is no end to Pendragon mysteries of crystal caves, or rood rings of an Eye of Fire, unveiled in the midst of ever-shining tors, here on Manstone Mynd.